Provincial Trade Wars: Why the Blockade Must End

edited by Filip Palda

THE FRASER INSTITUTE

The Fraser Institute, Vancouver, Canada

Printed in Canada.

Canadian Cataloguing in Publication Data

Main entry under title:

Provincial trade wars

Includes bibliographical references.
ISBN 0-88975-166-8

1. Interprovincial commerce—Canada. 2. Restraint of trade—Canada—Provinces. 3. Trade regulation—Canada—Provinces. 4. Nontariff trade barriers—Canada—Provinces. I. Palda, Filip (K. Filip) II. Fraser Institute (Vancouver, B.C.)
HF3226.5.P76 1994   381'.5'0971   C94-910079-X

Contents

Acknowledgements

I WANT TO THANK THE FOLLOWING PEOPLE for their kind help in bringing this book to completion: Larry J. Martin, Director of the George Morris Centre in Guelph, Peach Akerhielm, Manager of Policy and Planning, Industry, Science and Technology Canada in Vancouver. I also want to thank Marie Morris for fine administrative help, Kristin McCahon for her copy-editing and typesetting, and John Robson for his copy-editing. All three are with the Fraser Institute.

About the authors

Norman Bonsor is a Professor of Economics at Lakehead University and was educated at the University of Bradford (U.K.) and the University of Connecticut. He has written for the C.D. Howe Institute, the Economic Council of Canada, the Ontario Economic Council and the Royal Commission on the Economic Union and Development Prospects for Canada (McDonald Commission). He has authored a number of books and articles in academic journals dealing with transportation economics.

Morley Gunderson is the Director of the Centre for Industrial Relations and a Professor in the Department of Economics at the University of Toronto. He has a B.A. in Economics from Queen's University (1967) and an M.A. in Industrial Relations (1969) and a Ph.D. in Economics (1971) from the University of Wisconsin-Madison. During 1977/78 he was a Visiting Scholar at the International Institute for Labor Research in Geneva, Switzerland and during 1984/85 and 1991-93, he was a Visiting Scholar at Stanford University. His publications include books as well as numerous journal articles on various topics including: sex discrimination and comparable worth; public sector wages; the aging work force, pensions and mandatory retirement; and labour adjustment and free trade.

Ian Irvine is an Associate Professor of Economics at Concordia University. He studied for his Ph.D. at the University of Western Ontario. His earliest interests were in the distribution of income and wealth among households and in life cycle models. His interests have expanded to include consumer and taxation problems, the welfare cost of levying taxes, mortgage and housing demand, income uncertainty and, most recently, the alcoholic beverages sector of the economy. He has researched and written several papers in this area which have focused on scale economies in brewing, the effect of GATT rulings on the industry and on tax revenues from alcohol. His papers have appeared in the *Economic Journal*, the *Canadian Journal of Economics*, the *Quarterly Journal of Economics*, the *Journal of Public Economics* and others. Professor Irvine is a strong believer in the Friedman/Becker approach to economic policy making which emphasizes the essential role which markets can play.

Jean-Luc Migué is Professor of Economics at the School of Public Administration, in Quebec City. He is a graduate of the University of Montreal and received his Ph.D. from the American University, Washington, D.C. He specializes in the application of economic methods to government choices. He has written extensively in various issues of economic theory and policy. He has served as member of government task forces and as consultant for a number of organizations, active in the fields of education, environment and telecommunications. His current research interests include environmental problems and the impact on domestic policy choices of constraining the power of national governments to maintain trade barriers.

Filip Palda is Senior Economist at the Fraser Institute in Vancouver. He received his B.A. in 1983, and his M.A. in 1984 from Queen's University, Kingston. He continued his studies and in 1989 earned a Ph.D. in economics from the University of Chicago. His dissertation "Electoral Spending" was directed by Nobel laureate Gary S. Becker. From 1989 to 1991 Dr. Palda was professor of Economics at the University of Ottawa. He has published two books, *Election Finance Regulation in Canada: A Critical Review* and *Tax Facts Eight*, and has published numerous articles in refereed journals on the theory and measurement of political phenomena. He writes a syndicated column for the Sterling chain of newspapers and appears regularly in the media as an economic and political commentator.

Dr. John C. Pattison is Senior Vice-President, Compliance at Canadian Imperial Bank of Commerce, where he has previously held positions as Managing Director, CIBC Limited (London, England) and Vice-President, Finance. He has been at various times a Director of CIBC subsidiaries in Canada, England, France, the Channel Islands and Australia. He is currently a member of the Steering Committee on the reform of deposit insurance under the auspices of the Deputy Minister of Finance.

He is a former faculty member of the School of Business Administration, University of Western Ontario and was an economist at the O.E.C.D. in Paris, France. His books and articles have been published in Canada, the United States, Switzerland, Germany, Italy, the Netherlands and the United Kingdom. He is on the Board of Contributing Editors of *Canadian Financial Services Alert*.

Dr. Pattison's activities involve managing compliance risk on a global basis in order to ensure adherence to laws, regulations and the by-laws of self-regulatory bodies such as stock exchanges, in order to promote sound corporate governance of CIBC.

Dr. Barry E. Prentice, PhD, PAg, MCIT, was born and raised on a mixed farm at Port Perry, Ontario. He studied business administration and economics at the University of Western Ontario (B.A. 1974), and agricultural economics from the University of Guelph (M.Sc. 1979) and marketing and transportation at the University of Manitoba (Ph.D. 1986).

Since 1986, Dr. Prentice has held a joint appointment with the Transport Institute and Department of Agricultural Economics, University of Manitoba. His major research and teaching interests include logistics, transportation, agribusiness marketing, commercial policy, trade barriers, countertrade and export market development.

Dr. Prentice has authored or co-authored more than 75 journal articles, research reports and contributions to books. His scholarly work has been recognized for excellence in national paper competitions and awards.

He has served on the Boards of Directors of several non-profit organizations (Flax Council, CAPIC (Winnipeg Chapter), Canadian Transportation Research Forum, National Transportation Week) as well as government task forces and expert committees. Dr. Prentice has also served on trade missions to Southeast Asia and worked as a visiting professor at the Northwest Agricultural University, Xian, China.

William Sims is currently an Associate Professor in the Economics Department at Concordia University in Montreal, Quebec. He received his Ph.D at the University of Toronto in 1978. His primary area of research interest is applied microeconomics and, in particular, environmental economics, transportation economics, the economics of regulation and welfare economics. He has published papers in various journals, including the *Rand Journal of Economics*, the *Journal of Public Economics*, the *Review of Economics and Statistics* and the *Canadian Journal of Economics*.

Preface: Why Canada Must Rid Itself of Interprovincial Trade Barriers

Filip Palda

Needless harm to ourselves

INTERPROVINCIAL TRADE BARRIERS ARE PERHAPS the biggest solvable economic problem that our politicians cannot bring themselves to solve. These barriers cost Canadians at least $6.5 billion a year in lost income. The figure is that large because trade between the provinces is large. Statistics Canada records that in 1989 the provinces traded $146 billion worth of goods and services. This is only slightly less than the $160 billion dollars of trade Canadians did that year with the rest of the world (see Figure 1). We do not know precisely how much larger the internal market would be if goods and services could flow freely. What we do know is that internal barriers raise the cost of doing business, increase taxes, destroy jobs, and make us less competitive. By lessening each province's dependence on other provinces, barriers also work against Canadian unity.

Figure 1: Exports from Province to Province and from Province to Foreign Countries in 1989 (Billions of dollars)

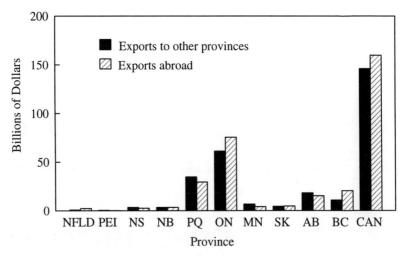

This book explains how interprovincial barriers produce these unfortunate effects.

Number and types of barriers

Until recently, no one had a precise idea of how many barriers to trade existed between provinces. A 1983 study by Trebilcock and his colleagues found hundreds. In 1992 Ottawa made a detailed study of the problem. The thousands of pages cataloguing barriers and describing their effects resemble the documents that Ottawa prepared for its negotiations with Mexico and the U.S. on the North American Free Trade Agreement.[1] This is no accident. Barriers may come down only after long and complicated talks between Ottawa and the provinces. Talks will be complicated because there are probably greater obstacles to trade

---

1   See for example the study on identifying interprovincial barriers, written by Smith Gunther and Associates Ltd. for the federal ministry of Industry, Science and Technology.

between the provinces than there are to trade between Canada and the rest of the world (Loizides and Grant 1992, p. 6).

Some barriers stand out. For example, until the fall of 1993 Alberta had an embargo on the export of liquid natural gas; rules in Ontario make it hard for out-of-province doctors to practice; Quebec forbids fish and crab caught in Quebec being processed in another province. It is harder to see how a standard for the length of trucks, a requirement that engineers and consultants receive provincial certification to practice, or a province's decision to buy domestic goods and services hurt trade. This is perhaps why these hidden barriers flourish. Standards and certification rules sound nice but can bring commerce to a halt. For example, a truck longer than the standard dictated by Ontario is not allowed to dock in Ontario. This raises transportation costs, and these costs are ultimately borne by the consumer. While it sounds patriotic for a provincial government to buy what it needs from residents, if those residents charge more than the residents of other provinces the government imposes an unnecessary tax burden on its citizens.

Perhaps the least obvious barriers are federal subsidies to depressed areas of the country and the corresponding high tax burden that other areas must bear. Subsidies encourage workers and businesses to ignore the economic call to move to other provinces. For example, during the 1960s workers were moving out of the Maritimes to seek better jobs elsewhere. This was a painful but necessary adjustment which eventually promised those workers better living conditions. As the Economic Council of Canada writes regarding this exodus "Overall, the pattern of provincial flows reveals that migration results in a significant amount of net labour-force redistribution, with labour supply shifting to regions with expanding employment and higher wages. This suggests that labour mobility in Canada probably makes a positive contribution to economic efficiency and provides workers with opportunities that would not otherwise be available in their home province."[2]

---

2   Somewhat cryptically in the same passage the Economic Council tempers this observation with the comment that "It would take further research, however to ascertain whether the new jobs pay better wages than the ones that are being left behind " (p. 43).

The trend in migration reversed suddenly in 1971; the year in which the Trudeau government reformed the UI Act to give a greater increase in benefits to provinces with the highest unemployment. As Figure 2 shows, between 1971 and 1981 workers flowed *back* into three of the four maritime provinces. The UI program was made slightly less generous in 1979. Net migration into the provinces stopped, but only Newfoundlanders have since chosen to resume the exodus.

Costs of barriers

Measuring the cost of barriers to Canadians is a vast and complicated task. To date we have only estimates, based on the observation that barriers impose administrative costs on businesses, keep industries too small to reap the cost advantages of large size, hide vital economic clues for consumers and producers, and impose hidden taxes on residents.

But we can see that they do have costs. Trade barriers drive a wedge between the true benefits of producing something and the benefits that people perceive. The many overlapping provincial and federal regulations a trust company in B.C. must obey in order to do business in Ontario may discourage the B.C. company from serving and satisfying

Figure 2:
Net Interprovincial Migration, Atlantic Provinces, 1961-91*

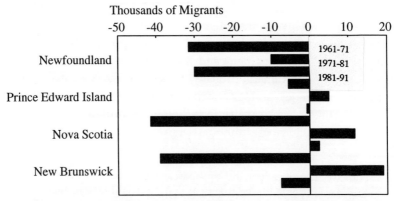

* The period covered extends from June 1, 1961 to May 31, 1991.

Source: Economic Council of Canada, 1991.

Ontario customers. Society loses because the government-made cost gets in the way of a fruitful exchange between producers and consumers. A federal subsidy to the Hibernia oil project off the coast of Newfoundland draws skilled labour, sophisticated equipment, and managerial talent away from the rest of Canada. These scarce resources are gambled on a venture which oil experts deem too foolish to risk without government backing. Society loses because the government subsidy encourages an exchange between producers of oil and future consumers which costs more than it is worth.

Certain types of trade barriers stunt the growth of industries. Until 1992 beer could be sold only in the province where it was brewed. This created beer jobs in every province but artificially raised the cost of beer. Canadian beer plants are less than one quarter the size of U.S. plants and Canadian wage costs are roughly double those of their U.S. counterparts per unit of product. Two or three large domestic breweries could have serviced the Canadian market at a fraction of the cost which ten small provincial breweries incurred. The Canadian beer industry must now suddenly recover from this inefficient style of operating if it wants to compete with the U.S.

The stunted size of the beer and many other industries lead to higher costs which are in the end passed on to consumers. A survey of 50 business by Loizides and Grant (1992) revealed that "In instances where a company uses a relatively large domestic market base to export, the existence of interprovincial barriers can also reduce the firm's international competitiveness" (pp. 5-6). In other words, by limiting their own market Canadians limit their ability to confront other countries on the international market.

Competitiveness is a big word which boils down to the ability to bring a sound product to the market at a price that consumers will pay. Being an efficient producer is only part of being competitive. The other part is knowing the market and informing the market of the product. Loizides and Grant found that barriers make it hard to develop such marketing strategies for the country: "This problem was mentioned most often by pharmaceutical manufacturers and retailers. The marketing impact is also seen in a tendency for firms to facing interprovincial trade barriers to replace national marketing programs with greater emphasis on marketing to the United States. Ironically, with the Canada-U.S. Free Trade Agreement (FTA), *many Canadian firms are facing fewer barriers to trade in the United States than they face in Canada* [my emphasis]" (p. 6).

Canada is still at the front of international competitors but it cannot afford to give up any advantage. We have had the second highest rate of growth of investment among G-7 countries over the last 30 years, we have created jobs faster than any G-7 country in the last thirty years, and we have the third highest level of labour productivity in the world after the United States and the Netherlands. We have done this in spite of the economic drag of barriers which raise the cost of producing and distributing goods. Without barriers we could well have the best economic performance.

Estimating the benefits of free internal trade

An optimistic estimate of the benefits of allowing firms to operate freely across the country is that the average Canadian family income would rise permanently by $3500 per year. This estimate comes from applying a study on European unification to Canada. The European study estimated that creating a free European market would raise average European incomes by at least 6.5 percent. The problem of such comparisons is that Canada and Europe have different geography and the people are distributed differently. An estimate of the gains from free internal trade for Europe may be higher if transportation costs are on average higher for Canada. A more conservative estimate for Canada is an permanent increase in income of 1.5 percent, a figure cited by the MacDonald Commission of the mid-1980s.

The benefits of removing certain barriers, such as preferential hiring and procurement practices, or provincial markups on alcohol and agricultural products, are easier to measure. Todd Rutley, of the Canadian Manufacturer's Association, estimated that these types of barriers cost Canadians $6.5 billion every year (Rutley, 1991). Rutley came to this figure by assuming that governments procure goods and services at a price on average 5 percent higher than the lowest possible cost, and then multiplying this overpayment by the amount spent on government procurement in 1990, which was $100 billion. He also estimated that provincial markups on alcohol and agricultural products cost consumers $1.5 billion more than they should be paying.

Perhaps the largest benefit, but also the most difficult to estimate, will come from the improved climate for business created by free internal trade. When in the mid 1980's Mexico decided to rejoin the world of international commerce it set off an economic boom. The same happened in several Latin American countries. Their economies boomed because investors came to believe that politicians were sincere about providing a stable, open climate for business. Canada is already a stable country, but it has a history of occasional government hostility to investors. Our severe Canadian content rules on producers and investors, and rising corporate tax burdens, are a sign of this hostility. An internal free trade agreement could erase part of this impression.

Non-benefits

Even though the federal government has worked hard to tell the public of the benefits of removing barriers, some of its arguments can be questioned. One commonly heard view is that removing barriers will allow governments to coordinate their activities and to supply goods more efficiently. An official document explains that "A major advantage of federalism (and one that is not available in less integrated forms of economic associations) is the opportunity it provides to co-ordinate and harmonize economic policies. Such policy coordination is essential for good economic performance since economic policies in one jurisdiction can have substantial economic effects on other jurisdictions" (*Partnership for Prosperity*, p. 13).

Harmony and policy coordination are hard to argue against unless one is aware that the great international cartels, such as OPEC, and the sugar and uranium cartels, are founded on harmony between governments. Ten provinces acting in harmony can act like a tax cartel by agreeing to uniformly high taxes across the country. If there is no agreement between the provinces to "harmonize" tax policies, then labour and capital can escape a province that levies high taxes and provides social services inefficiently. The labour and capital will settle in a province with more efficient government. If Canadians could vote with their feet in this manner they might force provincial governments to become more competitive.

Fear of such competition is perhaps behind the push by European government for political integration.

Barriers and jobs

The popular impression is that even though barriers increase costs for consumers, barriers at least preserve jobs. Similar arguments have been made concerning the free trade agreement with the U.S. and the NAFTA, so our experience with the U.S. free trade agreement can help to evaluate this claim. Daniel Schwannen of the C.D. Howe Institute has found that the economic sectors liberalized by the free trade agreement with the U.S. experienced increased growth (1993). Free trade has led to the creation of high-paying high value-added jobs. While "the net effect of the FTA so far has probably been slightly negative," the long-run effect will help industries which are vital to Canada's future to compete better. This will make Canadians on average richer and provide them with more secure employment.

The inference for interprovincial barriers is that they may stand in the way of high quality jobs. One reason our incomes have risen over the years is that each Canadian has more productive equipment and technologies to help them on their jobs. By keeping businesses too small to be fully efficient, and by forcing them to invest money in the administration necessary to deal with regulations, barriers leave workers with less capital than they could have to increase their productivity.

Political forces

The political reasons for ending barriers will depend only in part on a rational assessment of the economic benefits described above. Barriers will come down because of international pressures, and pressures by a few organized interest groups.

In negotiations for free trade, the free trade advocates tend to be only as powerful as the producers who back them. Consumers seldom have much say in the outcomes because it is in no individual consumer's interest to lobby the government. Average citizens have trouble seeing that regulations which increase the cost of trucking make their groceries cost more. Even if they knew about every barrier, they would shrug, because the several hundred dollars they would save each year would not outweigh the cost of lobbying politicians for change.

Producers, on the other hand, make their living from the regulated market and are well informed about it. The tension between producers can provide politicians with the impetus either to strike a barrier down or to keep it standing. A sign of such tension between producers came in September 1993 when the Ontario government complained to Quebec of rules that all but bar Ontario building-trades workers, construction contractors, and bus manufacturers from the Quebec market (*Globe and Mail*, p. A1, September 2, 1993). This followed on complaints and retaliations by certain Maritime provinces against Quebec. In other provinces it is also producers who are the main force lobbying against barriers.

Change is possible

Recently the federal government convinced the provinces to talk about internal free trade. In March of 1993 provincial ministers agreed to start "intensive negotiations toward a barrier-free Canadian market" and Ottawa appointed a chief internal trade negotiator (*Financial Post*, p. 7, August 6, 1993). The ambitious goal is to remove all barriers by the summer of 1994.

If these negotiations do not succeed then pressure to liberate internal trade will have to come from international agreements, court challenges, and public opinion. For example, in a 1991 GATT (General Agreement on Tariffs and Trade) panel ruling U.S. brewers successfully challenged restrictive provincial obstacles to their beer. Canadian and American governments signed an agreement to end Canadian discriminatory markups and taxes on imported beer by July 1992 and to allow imported beers equal access to retail shelves by October 1, 1993. This has forced the provincial governments to move away from the rule that a beer must be brewed in the province where it is sold, a rule which makes it impossible for Canadian brewers to build plants of a size necessary to compete with the U.S. Another example is the agricultural provisions of the proposed GATT. If the international community can agree on the GATT, Canadian dairy and poultry marketing boards will have to give up their restrictive practices, practices which include interprovincial restrictions on the food trade.

Court challenges may also threaten barriers. In 1989 a certified general accountant took P.E.I. to court because of a provincial law which allowed him to practice in New Brunswick but not in P.E.I. The accountant won on the grounds that the P.E.I. law violated his rights to mobility under the Charter of Rights and Freedoms. P.E.I. has appealed the case.

Purpose of this book

Public opinion is the last resort for moving governments to action, but to date public opinion has not been very strong on barriers, perhaps because few people understand the costs these barriers impose. There are even signs that many Canadians look with distrust on the removal of barriers. In 1991 early drafts of the proposed federal constitution had passages strongly advocating free internal trade. Under pressure from social activists the federal government softened its position and removed most mentions of an economically united Canada from later drafts.

The present book presents six essays that try to explain to a broad audience the costs of interprovincial trade barriers. Each essay analyses the effects of barriers on an particular industry or a broad segment of the economy.

Barriers to the movement of alcohol, particularly beer, are the subject of the essay by Professors Irvine and Sims. They explain that until recently beer had to be brewed in the province where it was sold. This left Canada with plants that are too small and as a result too expensive to operate in competition with American rivals. The threat of competition from the U.S. has forced the beer industry to become more efficient and to push provincial governments for a loosening of their regulation. The recent merger of Carling and Molson, which is a sign of the preparation for competition, will increase the industry's efficiency enormously. Irvine and Sims however, argue that ending the embargoes on the interprovincial movement of beer and other alcohols will not bring consumers the full benefits of free trade, unless certain provinces, such as Ontario and Quebec, also allow price competition in their province. This means an end to regulated price markups on alcoholic beverages.

Dr. John Pattison's essay gives us a clear look at the tangled world of financial regulation. He explains how the provinces prohibit or

severely limit the ability of residents to deal with institutions or salesmen in another province. A consumer who wants to deal with an
institution from out-of-province cannot even voluntarily decline the
protection of the province. As a result, writes Dr. Pattison, "a monumental interprovincial barrier to trade is created." For example, Ontario has
in place a regime of "Universal Registration" which forces anyone
selling securities to be regulated. Other provinces are less regulated and
more open. Ontario's regulations add an extra cost to selling securities
in the province. This discourages businesses from other provinces from
competing with local businesses. A refinement of the practice of imposing extra costs on outsiders is Ontario's "equals approach." This approach *requires any trust company operating in Ontario to comply with
Ontario regulations in all of its operations in other provinces, not just with
those in Ontario.* Dr. Pattison calls for an end to such restrictive regulation
and for less overlap in provincial and federal laws governing the financial sector. The European community has rid itself of such laws. If
Canadian financial institutions are to compete with the rest of the world,
they must be given the chance to practice at home.

Food products are the most traded goods among the provinces.
Professor Barry Prentice surveys the field of agricultural trade barriers.
He explains how quotas on dairy and poultry products have frozen the
pattern of agricultural production in Canada, how differing provincial
regulations on the packaging of basic food products has discouraged
trade, and how subsidies to farm production have prevented human
and physical resources from moving their most productive use. The
essay presents an in-depth history of the different types of provincial
barriers to agricultural trade and discusses the prospects for reform.

Transportation services are the most traded commodity within
Canada (Statistics Canada, *The Daily*, August 24 1993). Professor Norman C. Bonsor explains that much progress has been made toward
eliminating interprovincial barriers to transportation but that several
areas are still in need of reform. There is still the question of lack of
uniformity across Canada in maximum commercial vehicle length.
Fifty-three foot trailers are standard in western provinces and in all but
four U.S. states. Professor Bonsor argues that the 49 foot limitation in
Ontario and the Atlantic provinces raises the cost of interprovincial
highway movements. In the case of railways, restrictive labour legisla-

tion makes it difficult for new interprovincial shortline operators take up tracks formerly used by Canadian Pacific and Canadian Atlantic Railways. Such legislation will eventually lead to the wasteful abandonment of interprovincial trackage.

Professor Morley Gunderson presents an overview of barriers to the movement of labour. These barriers come in many forms: restrictive trade licences that specify that a professional must have trained in a province to practice there, procurement policies that lead to the hiring of local labour over out-of-province labour, and unemployment insurance which creates artificial incentives for labour to stay put in depressed areas. The essay explains that these barriers to labour mobility have immediate costs, but that they also have long term consequences. By preventing workers from moving to better quality jobs these barriers diminish the incentive to accumulate skills and training. An undertrained workforce will make it hard for Canada to compete in foreign markets.

Professor Jean-Luc Migué's essay puts interprovincial barriers in a larger context. He argues that free trade between the provinces has two benefits. First, trade stimulates competition between businesses. But second, trade also can force provincial governments to compete with each other to provide their residents with good quality social services at the lowest possible tax price. Provinces who do not compete vigorously may find that workers and capital flee to provinces which offer a better package. However, provincial governments will feel less pressure to compete with each other if the federal government insulates them from the consequences of ill-advised economic and social policies. For example, federal transfers to a province may hide from its residents the fact that the services they receive from the government are not good value for the level of tax they are paying. They only appear to be good value because of the federal subsidy which allows the provincial government to cover up its inefficiency. Residents of such provinces will not feel the need to move to other more efficient provinces. Professor Migué argues against federal government interference in provincial affairs, even if such interference appears to be helpful. His view that economic competition can lead to political competition deserves deeper consideration in the Canadian policy debate than it has received to date.

The industries discussed in this book are by no means the only ones to be affected by interprovincial barriers. Forestry, fishing, mining, energy, and pharmaceutical, to mention a few others, are also greatly affected. The goal of the essays in this book is to give the reader a sense of how interprovincial barriers can limit Canada's economic potential. The ideas developed here can serve as a guide when considering the effects of these other barriers on the economy.

References

Economic Council of Canada (1991). *A Joint Venture: Twenty-Eighth Annual Review*. Ottawa: Ministry of Supply and Services.

Loizides, Stelios, and Michael Grant (1992). "Barriers to Interprovincial Trade: Implications for Business." *Conference Board of Canada Report 93-92*.

Partnership for Prosperity (1991). *Canadian Federalism and Economic Union*. Ottawa: Ministry of Supply and Services.

Rutley, Todd (1991). "'Canada 1993': a Plan for the Creation of A Single Economic Market in Canada." *Canadian Manufacturer's Association Report on Interprovincial Trade*.

Smith Gunther and Associates Ltd. (1992). "Background Notes on the Identification of Interprovincial Non-Tariff Barriers." Working draft submitted to the Ministry of Industry, Science and Technology Canada.

Statistics Canada (1993). "Interprovincial Trade Flows of Goods and Services." *The Daily*, August 24, pp. 2-9.

Schwannen, Daniel (September, 1993). "A Growing Success: Canada's Performance under Free Trade." C.D. Howe Institute Commentary, no. 52.

Trebilcock, Michael J., John Whalley, Carol Rogerson, and Ian Ness (1983). "Provincially Induced Barriers to Trade in Canada: a Survey." In *Federalism and the Canadian Economic Union*, pp. 243-352. Edited by Michael J. Trebilcock, Robert S. Pritchard, Thomas

J. Courchene, and John Whalley. Toronto: Ontario Economic Council.

Interprovincial Barriers in the Beer Trade

**Ian J. Irvine and
William A. Sims
Department of Economics,
Concordia University**[1]

Introduction

THE RESTRUCTURING WHICH HAS BEEN UNDERWAY in the Canadian brewing industry for the last few years is arguably the most momentous in its history. It is attributable, on the one hand, to the power that

1   The authors are grateful to a number of people who either improved an earlier draft of this paper or provided them with information on the brewing industry in Canada and the U.S.: Kenneth Elzinga, Phil Katz, Marilyn Brophy, Ian De Verteuil, Brian Lomas, Earl New, Lorraine Elworthy, John Licharson, Fred O'Riordan, Bill Sharpe, and our editor Filip Palda. None of the above are in any way responsible for the views expressed in this paper.

governments in Canada have used to regulate the industry, and changes in the way such powers are being used. On the other, it is due to international trade pressures coming through the General Agreement on Tariffs and Trade (GATT) and to competitive pressures which spring from a market which has been stagnant for a decade. Moreover, while beer was exempted from the Canada-U.S. Free Trade Agreement (FTA), the belief that this will not remain so indefinitely has prompted the brewers to become more cost effective.

In this paper we will examine the impact of provincial governments on the industry: how their powers have caused serious inefficiencies; and how the use of these powers is evolving as a result of being challenged in the international arena through the GATT, and as a result of a federal government push to ensure a more open national market for Canadian industry.

Historically, the production, distribution, advertisement, sale and consumption of alcoholic beverages have been tightly regulated by both the federal and provincial governments. The current structure of the beer market—the number, location and size distribution of plants—is largely a function of these controls.

Government revenues from alcoholic beverages are considerable, accounting for 2.7 percent of total government tax revenues (Brewers Association of Canada, 1991). At present, federal and provincial government levies on beer for home consumption account for 53 percent of its price. From a total expenditure of $9.6 billion on beer consumed at and away from home in 1992, $3.1 billion went directly to governments (Brewers Association of Canada, 1993). This total does not include corporate and personal income tax revenues which also come from brewing industry operations.

The alcoholic beverages market is primarily under provincial jurisdiction. Federal powers are restricted to controls and taxes on production and importation. The *Federal Excise Act* governs the production of beer and spirits. It requires brewers, *inter alia,* to comply with bonding and licensing regulations and to pay specific taxes on their production. Wine is governed by the *Excise Tax Act*, more as a result of historical accident than of a policy decision to have a separate act. In addition to these excise levies, the federal government has two other sources of revenue from alcoholic beverages: the Goods and Services Tax (GST) and duties which, under the *Customs Tariff Act*, are imposed on imports. Additional duties are sometimes imposed on imports by, or on behalf of, provincial liquor boards.

The federal *Importation of Intoxicating Liquors Act* assigns to provincial governments, or their agents, the exclusive right to import liquor into the province, whether from outside the province or from another country. Provincial control is further assured through powers contained in various liquor control and licensing acts.

These powers have been used extensively, not only in brewing, but also in the wine and spirits segments of the alcoholic beverages industry. Indeed, while it is the effect of provincial authority on beer that has received most attention in the recent period, provincial governments have also implemented draconian measures in the wine sector in order to protect specific provincial interests, most notably in British Columbia, Ontario and Quebec.[2]

The reasons frequently given for restrictions on the production and sale involve social objectives such as promoting temperance, minimizing health costs, and reducing accidents and addiction. Such restrictions and their justification are mirrored in historical practice in Canada. For example, local jurisdictions were permitted to determine whether alcoholic beverages could be sold legally under the *Canada Temperance Act* of 1878. The result of this was to reduce the consumption of spirits drastically within a few decades and to double the consumption of beer.

Provincial governments generate considerably greater revenues from alcohol taxation than their federal counterparts. While the structure of charges varies by province there are again two major components: the provincial sales tax (PST) and what are referred to as "markups," usually *ad valorem*. In some provinces, particularly Quebec, a different charge is imposed, though its effect is similar to that of a markup.

---

2   In the wine industry, in addition to differential markups, specific rules favouring local segments of the industry have been in place for some time. In Ontario and British Columbia these rules have been in the form of a required minimum content of locally grown grapes in wine, and in Quebec that the wine sold in convenience stores be locally *bottled*. But, as with the beer industry, such practices are at present under scrutiny.

It is the imposition of differential markups on domestic and imported products by the provinces that has been a major factor in the rulings by the GATT against Canada.[3] In 1988 a GATT Panel found in favour of a complaint brought by the European Community (EC) that provincial policies discriminated against imported alcoholic beverages. A subsequent agreement was reached between the EC and Canada on liquor board practices which provided for national treatment in respect of listings, distribution and mark-up policies. A later GATT Panel report in 1991, which found in favour of a U.S. complaint, was directed squarely at provincial beer marketing practices. It enumerated areas where these practices were inconsistent with international trading rules, including: listings; retail point of sale; delivery and price structures—the last encompassing cost of service components, mark-up structures and minimum pricing.[4] A summary of such findings can be found in various recent issues of FOCUS.

The irony is that these practices by provincial governments have discriminated not only against foreign producers but equally against out of province domestic producers. Furthermore, these discriminatory practices have been compounded by production regulations, which have required that beer sold in any province be brewed in that province. Such requirements have not always been laid down in the form of legislation. Rather, the power derived from the *Intoxicating Liquors Act* enabled the provincial governments to demand local production— under the threat of legislation. As a consequence of such requirements, the industry has been forced into a production straightjacket, with attendant high costs and high prices to the consumer.

---

3   As an example of the importance of such differentials: until recently, Ontario had imposed a markup on beer produced in Ontario of 26 cents per litre, but on beer produced abroad *and* on beer produced out of province of 92 cents per litre.

4   Minimum pricing legislation involves the setting of a minimum retail price at which beer can be sold in various provinces. While such a law definitely restricts competition, as well as trade, it appears that at least 4 Canadian provinces (Ontario, Newfoundland, Nova Scotia and B.C.) will retain them. As well, minimum pricing was adopted in Quebec in November, 1993.

The reason that it was the brewing industry that became the subject of such laws lies in the historical control that the provinces have wielded over the industry. But, at the same time, it was not until recent decades that such production stipulations were necessary in order to maintain local production. Before the advent of preservatives, and before the arrival of the technology which brought scale economies with it, brewing was a relatively localised industry which had to sell its product within a short time. It was only when the economies of large scale brewing became evident that firms saw an economic advantage to centralising production and that the provincial governments began to pressure the big brewers to produce in the province of sale. As we shall detail in this essay, the big brewers in Canada do not view the abolition of these production location regulations without some fear. While the centralization of brewing will undoubtedly increase efficiency, if this also means that Canada becomes more open to competition from U.S. producers, they may face a smaller market share and declining profitability.

Negotiations aimed at removing the interprovincial restrictions on the movement of beer have been underway since 1987 and agreement has already been reached on the part of several provinces regarding certain aspects of these barriers. The negotiations are complex for a number of reasons, not least of which is the differences in regulations across provinces.[5] In addition, the cost of such an agreement will vary widely across provinces due to differences in the relative size of employment and tax bases associated with the location of the brewing industry in a given region. Thus all provinces may not wish to see the same set of changes implemented. Because of this, any agreement reached on the abolition of interprovincial trade barriers will likely not involve all provinces. Even in those provinces that have reached such an agreement, particular regulations governing certain aspects of industry trade

---

5   The existence of different provincial regulations springs in part from the differences in the way beer is sold in each province. For example, in British Columbia beer is sold both through government-owned outlets and through privately owned stores, while in Ontario beer is sold almost exclusively through the Brewer's Warehousing Company (also known as the Brewer's Retail).

will continue to exist. Such details are described in section 5 of this paper for Ontario and Quebec. The important point to recognize at this juncture is that even if most provinces agree to lift restrictions on the location of brewing, this will not be equivalent to a blanket lifting of all barriers to out of province and out of country producers and will not place them on an equal footing with producers located in that province, or with producers who may obtain special status in selling in that province. The remaining barriers to competition, which we also detail later, spring both from a concern to maintain domestic (and provincial) employment, and from a successful effort by the major brewers in Canada to have their views represented in legislation.

The merger which took place between Molson and Carling-O'Keefe in 1989 was in part induced by these interprovincial barriers to the shipment of beer. Each had excess capacity in several plants across Canada, but they were prevented from reducing the high production costs associated with this because of the provincial requirements to maintain production in each province. The merger allowed Molson to reduce excess capacity in selected provinces and utilize capacity more fully in those same provinces, while at the same time increasing industry concentration. While this merger has led to increased rationalization of the production structure within provinces, and has undoubtedly improved cost effectiveness, it has not induced rationalization at the *national* level. Rationalization at the national level, which may be a source of equally large efficiency gains (Irvine *et al*, 1990), will only come about once the removal of interprovincial trade barriers is completed.

An important question is whether or not these cost reductions will be passed along to consumers. Indeed, the 1989 merger, and resulting increase in concentration, could reduce the already minimal domestic competitive pressures in the brewing industry and thus further reduce the possibility that consumers will face lower prices. How serious a problem this will be depends upon the degree to which competitive forces can be reintroduced into the marketplace. We shall argue later that there are reasons to be concerned about this possibility.

The structure of production in Canada and the U.S.

The structure of the Canadian brewing industry is a result of the historic limitations on competition sanctioned by government policies. The key policies which have had this effect involve limitations of trade, both interprovincial and international, and government policy towards mergers. The early structure of the industry was conditioned by a wave of mergers from the 1930s to the 1960s. Jones (1967) describes this movement as an attempt by the Big Three: Canadian Breweries (later Carling-O'Keefe), Labatt and Molson, to increase market power. As he concluded:

> It is clear that on economic grounds, unwarranted market power exists in the Canadian brewing industry, the Big Three seemingly have reached a position of permanence. The basis of this power is the acquisition process in which the Big Three engaged . . . (p. 568).

For example, in the period from 1930 to 1953 Canadian Breweries purchased more than 35 breweries (Jones, 1967, pp. 554-5). It does not appear that this merger movement lead to significant rationalization, since in 1926 there were 63 plants in Canada and by 1955 this number had become 59.

By 1960, Carling-O'Keefe held 49.1 percent of the domestic market and the Big Three combined had over 90 percent of the market. The industry had reached an unprecedented level of concentration, which has even increased slightly to the present day. The "position of permanence" that Jones hypothesized for the Big Three has however, proven elusive. From 1960 until the Molson Carling merger, Labatt's and Molson's market shares rose at the expense of Carling-O'Keefe. By the early 1980s Carling-O'Keefe's market share was down to under 25 percent, but the Big Three's share was above 97 percent (Goldberg and Eckel, 1983 p. 137).[6]

---

6   In 1992 Molson's share of the Canadian market was 51.7 percent and Labatt had a 42.3 percent share (Lomas, 1992). Thus the Big Two controlled 94 percent of the market, down slightly from 97 percent in the early '80s. By comparison the 2, 3 and 5 firm concentration ratios in the U.S. in 1991 were

The 1989 Molson-Carling-O'Keefe merger was accepted by government authorities as a method of rationalizing the industry, which until then had been prevented by interprovincial trade barriers. Such horizontal mergers tend to reduce competition and also reduce costs if there are economies of large scale production[7] or excess capacity.[8] This merger would be acceptable provided the cost reductions of the latter effects outweigh the efficiency losses from the former.[9] As well, distribution and marketing economies may result at the *firm* level if these costs do not increase proportionately with production and can thus be spread over a larger volume of output.

At the time of the merger both firms together were operating 16 plants, whereas by 1992 Molson (the name for both after the merger) was operating 9 plants. This trend towards rationalization has been

---

68.5 percent, 78.7 percent and 91.9 percent (Sfiligoj, 1992, p. 15).

7   Plant level economies of scale occur if unit costs decline with output as plant size increases. Rationalization of production involves closing down some plants in order to produce more output in larger plants, presumably at lower costs. A trend toward rationalization would be expected in any industry in which plants are operating at sub-optimal scale (i.e. at outputs which do not minimize unit costs) and in which scale economies are such that significant unit cost reductions would result from expanded plant output. Failure of an industry to rationalize in such circumstances provides *prima facia* evidence of the lack of vigorous competitive pressures.

8   Prior to the merger the capacity utilization rates for Molson and Carling-O'Keefe were 68 percent and 57 percent, respectively (Conference Board, 1990). After the merger this rose to around 87 percent.

9   Such a condition was ruled out for the early merger movement by Jones (1967). Since current scale economies at the plant and firm levels may have resulted from technological changes in bottling and canning, as well as from changes in media communications, it is arguable that the early merger movement was economically unjustified, while the 1989 Molson merger is acceptable on efficiency grounds. Elzinga (1990) notes that "the newer bottling lines at the Anheuser-Busch Houston brewery have line speeds of 1,100 bottles per minute. Modern canning lines are even faster: 2,000 cans per minute. It takes breweries of substantial size to utilize such equipment at capacity."

Empirical evidence on the advantages of rationalization of the Canadian brewing industry is discussed in the next section of this paper.

taking place for sometime. In 1957 there were 55 brewing plants operating in Canada and only 2 of these had capacities in excess of one million hectolitres per year. By 1981 there were 41 plants, 8 with capacities above one million hectolitres per year (Anastasopoulos, Irvine and Sims, 1986). By 1992 there were 32 conventional breweries with 7 having capacities in excess of one million hectolitres and 4 in excess of 2 million hectolitres.[10] The recent trend in plant numbers in Canada is shown in Table 1.

This process has been even more dramatic in the United States, largely due to the absence of interstate barriers to trade, as well as technological and media changes, that have expanded the minimum efficient scale of the plant and firm. In 1959 there were 203 brewing plants in the U.S. with only 2 having a capacity in excess of 4 million hectolitres. By 1986 there were 67 plants, 23 of which had capacities in excess of 4 million hectolitres (Elzinga, 1990).[11] Possibly more revealing

---

10   Elzinga (1990) argues that plant costs decline fairly sharply until a plant capacity of 1.5 million Hl. and continue to decline, but somewhat less sharply, until a capacity of 5.25 million Hl. Smith and Sims (1985) suggest that scale economies still exist at 3 million Hl. Of the 21 plants still operated by the big 2 in Canada in 1992, only 6 have capacities above 1.7 million Hl. While these are the largest plants in the country, it seems doubtful that they all have exhausted plant scale economies. Indeed, once advertising and distribution economies are considered it has been suggested that ". . . a competitive capacity, or critical mass . . . for a brewing *firm* in the U.S. market may currently be in the range of 25 to 28 million Hl" (Wolf, 1991, p.21). Only 3 firms in North America fulfil this requirement: Anheuser-Busch (A-B) with a capacity of 105 million Hl.; Miller with a capacity of 53 million Hl.; and, Coors with a capacity of 27 million Hl. Molson has a current capacity of 13.5 million Hl., sixth behind A-B, Miller, Coors, Stroh and Heileman. Partly as a result of these size discrepancies and economies of size, marketing costs for the Big Two in Canada amount to $25 per Hl., whereas in the U.S. the equivalent measure for A-B is $9 per Hl. (Lomas, 1992).

11   These figures, like those in Table 1, do not include breweries with capacities of less than 10,000 barrels (i.e. approximately 11,700 hectolitres (Hl.)). This excludes microbreweries. While this sector has grown numerically in recent years, it still provides insignificant brewing capacity and hence insignificant competition to *conventional* breweries in North America.

Table 1: Evolution of Brewing Plants in Canada

PROV.	FIRM	78	79	80	81	82	83	84	85	86	87	88	89	90	91	92
Nfld.	Carling	1	1	1	1	1	1	1	1	1	1	1	1	1	0	0
	Labatt	2	2	2	2	2	1	1	1	1	1	1	1	1	1	1
	Molson	1	1	1	1	1	1	1	1	1	1	1	1	1	1	1
	Total	4	4	4	4	4	3	3	3	3	3	3	3	3	2	2
N.S.	Labatt	1	1	1	1	1	1	1	1	1	1	1	1	1	1	1
	Other	1	1	1	1	1	1	1	1	1	1	1	1	1	1	1
	Total	2	2	2	2	2	2	2	2	2	2	2	2	2	2	2
N.B.	Labatt	1	1	1	1	1	1	1	1	1	1	1	1	1	1	1
	Other	1	1	1	1	1	1	1	1	1	1	1	1	1	1	1
	Total	2	2	2	2	2	2	2	2	2	2	2	2	2	2	2
P.Q.	Carling	1	1	1	1	1	1	1	1	1	1	1	1	0	0	0
	Labatt	1	1	1	1	1	1	1	1	1	1	1	1	1	1	1
	Molson	1	1	1	1	1	1	1	1	1	1	1	1	1	1	1
	Total	3	3	3	3	3	3	3	3	3	3	3	3	2	2	2
Ont.	Carling	1	1	1	1	1	1	1	1	1	1	1	1	1	1	1
	Labatt	3	3	3	3	3	3	3	3	3	3	3	3	3	3	3
	Molson	2	2	2	2	2	2	2	2	2	2	2	2	2	1	1
	Other	5	5	5	5	5	5	5	6	8	6	6	9	5	5	5
	Total	11	11	11	11	11	11	11	12	14	12	12	15	11	10	10
Man	Carling	1	1	1	1	1	1	1	1	1	1	1	1	1	1	1
	Labatt	1	1	1	1	1	1	1	1	1	1	1	1	1	1	1
	Molson	1	1	1	1	1	1	1	1	1	1	1	1	1	0	0
	Total	3	3	3	3	3	3	3	3	3	3	3	3	3	2	2
Sask.	Carling	2	2	2	2	2	1	1	1	1	1	1	1	0	0	0
	Labatt	1	1	1	1	1	1	1	1	1	1	1	1	1	1	1
	Molson	2	2	2	2	2	2	2	2	1	1	1	1	1	1	1
	Other	0	0	0	0	0	0	0	0	0	0	0	0	1	1	1
	Total	5	5	5	5	5	4	4	4	3	3	3	3	3	3	3

Table 1: Evolution of Brewing Plants in Canada

PROV.	FIRM	78	79	80	81	82	83	84	85	86	87	88	89	90	91	92
Alta.	Carling	1	1	1	1	1	1	1	1	1	1	1	1	1	1	1
	Labatt	1	1	1	1	1	1	1	1	1	1	1	1	1	1	1
	Molson	2	2	2	2	2	2	2	2	2	2	2	2	2	1	1
	Other	1	1	1	1	1	1	1	1	1	2	2	2	1	1	1
	Total	5	5	5	5	5	5	5	5	5	6	6	6	5	4	4
B.C.	Labatt	2	3	3	3	3	2	2	2	2	2	2	2	2	2	2
	Molson	1	1	1	1	1	1	1	1	1	1	1	1	1	1	1
	Carling	1	1	1	1	1	1	1	1	1	1	1	1	1	0	0
	Other	2	1	1	1	1	1	1	3	4	3	3	3	2	2	2
	Total	6	6	6	6	6	5	5	7	8	7	7	7	6	5	5
Can-ada	Big 3	31	32	32	31	31	29	29	29	28	28	28	28	26	21	21
	Total	41	41	41	41	41	38	38	41	43	41	41	44	37	32	32

Note: "Big 3" indicates Carling, Labatt, and Molson. "Other" includes all other breweries in the provinces other than the Big 3.

---

is the fact that the American brewing giants, Anheuser-Busch and Miller, operate 17 plants with *average* capacity of over 8 million Hl. (Elzinga, 1990 p.140). The largest Canadian brewer, Molson, operates 9 plants with an average capacity of slightly less than 1.5 million Hl. (Molson's Annual Report, 1992).[12] Tables 2 and 3 show the trend toward larger more efficient plants in the U.S. and to a lesser extent in Canada. Most of these recent changes in Canada have resulted from the 1989 merger.

The dispersed Canadian population, along with significant inter-provincial trade barriers, has prevented rationalization to the extent observed in the U.S.[13] The increasing threat of free trade with the U.S.

---

12   The largest Canadian plant is located in Montreal and is owned by Molson. It has a capacity of about 4 million Hl.

13   A Conference Board study suggests that rationalization, even in the pres-

has, however, provided an impetus for rationalization in Canada and for interprovincial free trade in beer—a necessary condition for full rationalization. In recent years the export market has been important for Canadian brewers, making up 11 percent of demand in 1990[14] (Brewers Association of Canada, 1990), with almost all of these exports going to the U.S. Imports, on the other hand, have been a relatively unimportant source of competition. Increasing trends towards free trade in North America, along with American complaints through GATT about unfair trade practices in the various Canadian provinces, may soon change this situation.[15]

This move towards free trade in beer has concerned domestic brewers, since Canadian plants are less than one quarter the size of U.S. plants and Canadian wage costs have been reported to be roughly double those of their U.S. counterparts per unit of product (Brewers Association of Canada, 1986). In 1992 the largest Canadian brewer, Molson, was the 6th largest in North America, with slightly more than 4 percent of this market. This compares with a market share of about 41 percent for the largest U.S. brewer: Anheuser-Busch. Indeed one American brewer produced just under 8 percent of U.S. demand in 1985, from

---

ence of interprovincial free trade, may continue to proceeded slowly because of "sunk fixed costs" in existing plants and the high capital costs of new plants. This argument (discussed in more detail in section 3) however, fails to explain U.S. trends.

14   Domestic sales in Canada have been flat at around 20 million hectolitres since the mid-1970s and are projected to decline to around 18 million hectolitres by 1996 (Lomas, 1992). Virtually all growth in sales for Canadian breweries in the last 2 decades has come from exports to the U.S. A recent GATT ruling on U.S. discriminatory practices against imports, which the U.S. government has accepted, bodes well for future growth of Canadian exports. The recently announced relationship between Miller and Molson should further enhance the market position of Canadian brewers in the U.S. market.

15   In the early '80s imports accounted for about 1 percent of the Canadian market, but by 1989 they made up 2.7 percent. This number increased to 4.5 percent in 1990 and is projected to grow to 6.5 percent by 1996 (Lomas, 1992). This growth in imported beer is projected to come mainly from the U.S.

Table 2: Capacity of U.S. Brewing Plants

Listed Capacity (1000s barrels)	1963	1967	1971	1975	1979	1983	1986
10 - 100	54	36	21	10	10	15	13
101 - 500	72	44	33	19	13	12	8
501 - 1000	33	35	32	13	8	2	3
1001 - 2000	17	18	21	13	11	13	10
2001 - 4000	10	10	12	12	13	9	10
4001+	3	4	7	15	20	23	23

Source: K. G. Elzinga (1990).

Table 3: Capacity of Canadian Plants Owned by the Big Three*

Listed Capacity (1000s barrels)	1982	1984	1988	1992
0 - 250	7	4	2	1
251 - 500	10	10	10	8
501 - 1000	7	7	7	5
1001 - 2000	5	4	4	3
2001 - 4000	3	4	5	4

*This was, of course, the Big Two in 1992.

Source: McCullough and McCafferty (1982); Food in Canada (1989); Molson's Annual Report (1992).

a single plant operation. This plant had a capacity equal to 75 percent of total Canadian consumption (Brewers Association of Canada, 1987).[16]

16 Coors produces in a single plant in Golden, Colorado. In 1991 its share of the U.S. market had increased to 10.2 percent or about 22.6 million Hl. (Sfiligoj, 1992). Total Canadian beer sales (including imports) in 1991 were just slightly in excess of 21 million Hl. (Lomas, 1992).

In addition, as has been pointed out by the president of the Brewers Association of Canada (1987):

> U.S. plants are currently operating at 75 percent capacity. Their total surplus would be enough to meet Canadian demand three times over.

The growth of American-produced beer in the Canadian market will likely come about, not solely because of the superior efficiency of U.S. production, but as a result of increased access to Canadian markets. In response to a 1991 GATT panel ruling against discriminatory trade practices by Canada, the American and Canadian governments signed an agreement to end Canadian discriminatory markups and taxes on imported beer by July, 1992, and to allow imported beers equal access to retail shelves by Oct. 1, 1993.[17] But it was also agreed at that time that certain provinces (Ontario, B.C., Newfoundland and New Brunswick) would retain their legislated minimum price regimes. This could imperil price competition in these jurisdictions and thus, at least for the time being, limit the growth of American brands.

Nevertheless, the threat of competition by a large and efficient adversary has induced several recent cost-cutting reactions in Canada: the Molson-Carling merger and subsequent rationalization; the expected plant closures by Labatt;[18] a move to standardized bottles; and major reductions in marketing costs. However, full industry rationalization can only take place once interprovincial free trade becomes a reality.

Measuring the economic impact

There are three recent studies which quantify the effects of removing interprovincial trade barriers in brewing. These are: The Conference Board of Canada's *An Assessment of the Impacts of Liberalised Interprovin-*

---

17   Since this agreement Ontario has moved this date up to the summer of 1993, while simultaneously imposing additional taxes on beer that impact most severely on imports.

18   Labatt's Waterloo plant is scheduled to close in 1993. As well, Scotia-McLeod forecasts the closure of Labatt's Saskatchewan plant by 1994 and its New Brunswick plant in 1995 (Lomas, 1992).

cial Trade in Canada (1990), Irvine, Sims and Anastasopoulos's *Interprovincial versus International Free Trade: The Brewing Industry* (1990) and *The Cost of Scale Inefficiency in the Canadian Brewing Industry* (1990), by Tsiritakis, Campbell and Merikas. These studies all reach the same general conclusions on the impact of eliminating the existing production rules, and their focus is upon benefits which would accrue under different *production rationalization* scenarios.

The reasons for gains are straightforward: (i) with the closure of some plants, fuller capacity utilization without any capital expansion could increase productivity and profitability, and (ii) the replacement of smaller plants by larger plants would strengthen this process, given scale economies.

The Conference Board report tends to concentrate somewhat more upon the benefits which accrue under rationalizing production in existing plants (i.e. increasing capacity utilization), whereas Irvine *et al* and Tsiritakis *et al* focus upon the gains over an assumed longer time period (i.e. from economies of scale and scope).[19] In examining the gains to freer trade among provinces we stress again that these studies have mirrored public debate and government concerns in focusing upon removing barriers to the *production location* of brewing. While this will bring major benefits, it still represents a limited form of liberalization.

Conference Board Study

The Conference Board undertook its study when the merger between Molson and Carling-O'Keefe took place. As noted above, one of the motivations for this partnership was the existence of excess capacity in each firm. Labatt, in contrast, appeared to be operating much closer to its capacity level than either of the new partners. With the closure of several plants, the Conference Board argued that the additional efficiency gains from further rationalization, following the removal of interprovincial barriers, would be minimal.

---

19 Economies of scope refer to the existence of cost complementarities from producing different products together, such that it is cheaper to produce several commodities in a single facility than to do so in separate facilities. Tsiritakis *et al* find no evidence of economies of scope in brewing.

The Conference Board commissioned some econometric work to examine the existence of scale economies. Using data for 32 plants in Canada, a cost function was estimated which related variable costs to output, capital, and direct and indirect wage costs. Having grouped the firms into small, medium and large categories the study concluded that the returns to scale[20] were similar across groups: broadly, a doubling of all inputs would increase output by between 129 percent and 138 percent. Figure 1 below is taken from the Conference Board report. It indicates that cost reductions tend to taper off when plant size reaches about two and a half million hectolitres. However, the findings rather surprisingly indicate that returns to scale are essentially the same regardless of whether a firm has a one million or two million hectolitre capacity.

The econometric work in the report is characterised by many statistically insignificant coefficients, and the methodology is not clearly outlined. This indicates that some caution should be exercised in adopting these results for policy analysis. In particular, the returns to scale for high output plants are much greater than those reported in Sims and Smith (1985).[21]

The question of why the industry would not immediately build a series of plants after the removal of interprovincial trade barriers, each producing two to three million hectolitres to take advantage of these scale economies, is answered in the Conference Board report by noting the difference between the long and short run, or between fixed and variable costs. An essential characteristic of brewing, it is argued, is that

---

20　It is not obvious, from the Conference Board study, how inferences on returns to scale can be drawn based on what appears to be a 'restricted' or short-run cost function. The co-efficient on output in their cost function appears to show how variable costs vary with output, given a fixed capital stock. This methodology has been used to estimate plant capacities, given data on the user cost of capital (Berndt and Hesse, 1986), but the Conference Board does not do this.

21　The latter reported a scale elasticity based on the estimation of a long-run cost function for brewing of 1.14 for the largest plant in their sample. This contrasts with an estimate of 1.38 for plants of comparable size in the Conference Board study.

Figure 1: Variable Cost of Production in Brewing

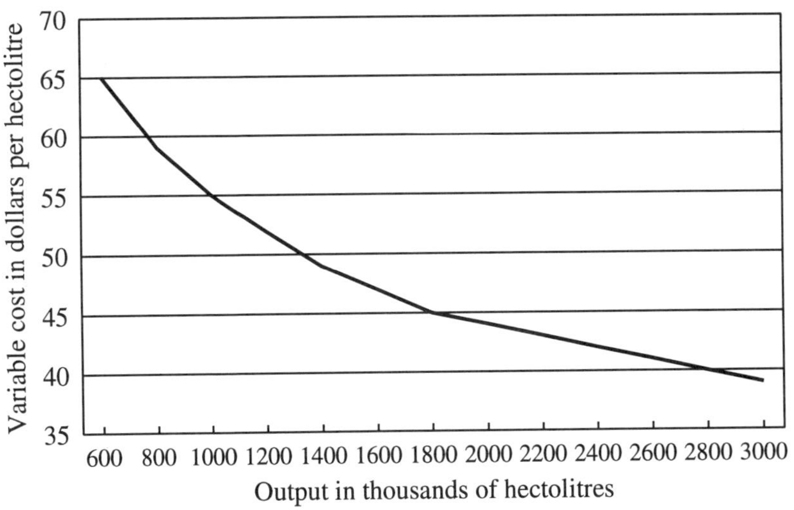

Source: Conference Board of Canada, 1990.

the capital in existing plants is sunk and durable. Consequently, it may not be profitable to invest in new capital before depleting the existing stock.[22] As a result, the Conference Board study concluded that, beyond the Molson-Carling merger, abolishing the interprovincial barriers to shipping beer across provincial boundaries would have only moderate effects on the structure, and hence on the efficiency and profitability of the industry. Thus full rationalization would only develop slowly.

This conclusion, in hindsight, is open to question. Since the merger, Labatt appears to have embarked upon its own restructuring program.[23]

---

22   If all the capital costs of an existing brewery are sunk, then a proposed new brewery will only be brought on line to replace the old brewery when its variable costs are below those of the old brewery by more than the annualized capital costs of the new facility. Of course for all of the capital costs of the old brewery to be sunk, the facility must have no alternative use or scrap value—a very stringent condition.

23   The problem noted in the Conference Board study explains why capital does not necessarily become obsolete immediately after the discovery of a

It appears to us that the key factor in the removal of interprovincial barriers is that this move is associated, in the view of the producers, with the potential for real competition from cost-effective producers in the U.S. While the optimal result for the domestic producers would be to insulate the Canadian market from such competition, the Big Two have seen the advent of freer trade in Canada as a signal to arm for battle in at least some of the provinces. With interprovincial barriers in place, the major producers could afford to continue producing in "inefficient" plants, because their profit margin was being protected by provincial controls on the industry.[24] But with effective competition in at least some provinces on the horizon, signalled by the prospective dismantling of barriers within Canada, the producers can no longer afford the luxury of continuing to produce in suboptimally sized plants, even if a "premature" move to larger plants squeezes profits in the short run.

Essentially, the competitive paradigm may not always be capable of explaining firm behaviour—especially in a protected industry: protection may foster high costs, and management may not feel the pressure to increase efficiency, provided the return on their capital is at least on par with that in the economy. However, if competition were to reduce such returns, then firms may be forced to remove this type of X-inefficiency.[25] To the extent that the Conference Board did not foresee

---

new, more efficient (i.e. lower variable costs) technology. Everyone did not rush out and scrap their 80386-based microcomputer immediately upon the marketing of a new, improved and faster 486-based clone. The same is true in brewing: old, inefficient plants still exist despite improvements in brewing and packaging technology and will do so for some time to come. The U.S. market has, however, also been subject to this structural phenomena, yet rationalization has continued there, and has done so despite more stringent antitrust laws than exist in Canada. One should thus not overestimate the significance of sunk costs, or underestimate the role of the regulatory blunting of competitive pressures, in explaining the current Canadian market structure.

24   For example, Brophy (1993) claims that Labatt is currently the most profitable brewer in North America, when measured per hectolitre of beer produced. She also predicts an increase in profitability as a result of rationalization.

25   X-inefficiency refers to managerial inefficiency which, as is pointed out by

any behavioral changes on the part of producers, it has underestimated the ultimate significance of the removal of the provincial restrictions on the structure of this industry.

Irvine, Sims and Anastasopoulos

The study by Irvine, Sims and Anastasopoulos (1990) computed the benefits of removing both the interprovincial and international trade barriers (in sequence). They focused upon the long run, that is, on a period long enough for existing capital in suboptimally sized plants to be depleted. The authors propose that the industry could then produce the existing output in about 12 plants, without significantly adding to the cost of transportation. Using cost function estimates from Sims and Smith (1985), which are based upon a time series of data for a small number of plants, yet include capital costs, they conclude that efficiency gains could amount to 30 percent of the existing costs of production.[26] These gains

> vary extensively by area, since the returns to scale vary with output. Thus, in consolidating the Prairie plants, the [unit] cost reduction is much greater than in Quebec, since the existing output per plant is much greater in Quebec.

The authors then examine how these gains might be apportioned between consumers and producers in the context of a further opening

---

Leibenstein (1966), "depends on the degree of competitive pressure, as well as on other motivational factors." He continues: "In situations where competitive pressure is light, many people will trade the disutility of greater effort, of search, and the control of other people's activities for the utility of feeling less pressure and of better interpersonal relations." Such X-inefficiency, in an industry which has been insulated from competition, may provide a good explanation of developments in the Canadian brewing industry.

26 An approximate dollar value of these gains would be 30 percent of one quarter of total expenditure on beer or about $750 million in 1992. This is based on the assumption that governments' and vendors' revenues make up about half of total expenditures, with the remaining half divided between production, on the one hand, and advertising, marketing, distribution, etc. on the other.

of the industry to foreign beer. They examine a variety of scenarios which depend upon the pricing behaviour of participants in the market, and whether the present production of "franchised" beer would be transferred back to U.S. plants or stay in Canada.

These gains are measured as the sum of changes in domestic consumer and producer surpluses.[27] Such total gains, however, do not accrue equally to producers and consumers. The authors argue that, given the oligopolistic structure of the industry, *international* free trade may be required to ensure that the potential gains from production rationalization are shared with consumers. But the effects of international free trade might *reduce* producer surplus, thus reducing the total gain to the economy, measured as the sum of domestic consumer and domestic producer gains. This may occur because, they hypothesize, the production of franchised beer could ultimately move back to parent plants in the U.S.

> Given the substantial scale economies, this marginal production is very profitable to the Canadian brewers. Thus, even if Canadian producers were to respond in the international free trade situation by reducing price, in an attempt to increase their market share, the resultant gain in consumer surplus would be offset by losses to the producers—primarily because of the inelastic demand for beer.[28]

The Irvine, Sims, Anastasopoulos study is set in a *long run* context and it does not address how the ownership of a greatly reduced number of plants would evolve, nor the magnitude of any additional transportation costs which might be associated with such a new pattern of production. However, as we shall argue below, their emphasis upon the joint role of interprovincial and international free trade is more import-

---

27 Producer surplus is the difference between the amount producers receive for a product and the minimum amount they would be willing to accept to supply the same quantity of that product. Consumer surplus is the difference between the maximum amount consumers are willing to pay for a product and the amount they actually pay.

28 Another way of viewing the loss in producer surplus is to recognize that there is a rent to the resources used in beer production which need not exist with the switch of these resources to another sector of the economy.

ant than even they may have recognized at that time. That is, even if additional transportation costs were associated with their hypothesised long run scenario, the effects of international competition may have additional impacts on the industry that, in efficiency terms, could be of a similar order of magnitude to the production gains examined.

Tsiritakis, Campbell and Merikas

Tsiritakis, Campbell and Merikas (1990) likewise address the issue of scale economies while at the same time examining the role of the multi-product production process. The objective of the latter examination is to see if the data indicate the presence of cost complementarities. They analyze the cost of producing three different products—bottled, canned and draught beer—in 25 different plants over the period 1978-82, by estimating a quadratic multi-product cost function. Their findings are that (1) unit costs are decreasing in all plants except the very largest in their sample (2) there exist differences in the fixed cost components of producing the three products and (3) cost complementarities in the production process do not seem to be present. Their estimate of the benefits of reducing plants from their 1978-82 numbers to about ten is 6.5 percent of production cost—a number far below the estimates of the Conference Board and Irvine *et al*. Without discussing their methodology, it is worth stating that the assumptions these authors impose on their model of the brewing process are quite severe, and these probably account for the fact that their estimates are at variance both with the other studies and with the observed practice of brewers to build ever larger breweries.

The efficiency fallout: governments and producers

The public debate on the removal of interprovincial barriers in the brewing industry has focused upon cost reductions following restructuring and upon the ability of the industry to compete more effectively against foreign producers. From the perspective of governments—both federal and provincial—an important element in this area is the manner in which their revenues from the industry are likely to respond to such changes. Were this any other sector of the economy, with perhaps the exception of tobacco, tax revenue effects would be a minor concern. But given the magnitude of such revenues, it is important that the probable changes be assessed.

A precise estimate of the effects of restructuring on producer prices, government revenues and producer revenues at the present time is somewhat speculative. This is because little can be inferred from the review of minimum pricing currently underway. Nonetheless, what is feasible is an analysis of how price reductions could affect these revenues.

We have used the Revenue Canada model for **G**overnment and **I**ndustry **R**evenue from **A**lcoholic **B**everages in **CAN**ada, GIRAB-CAN, (Irvine and Sims, 1991) to simulate the effects of changes in producer prices for the province of Ontario.

GIRAB-CAN is a demand model of the alcoholic beverages sector which disaggregates the three broad beverage groups into domestic and imported components. We have simulated the model for the province of Ontario by assuming that the producer price of domestically brewed beer could fall by 10 percent in a "rationalized" world. A feature of the model is that it has a matrix of cross price elasticities embedded within it.[29] This means that the effects of beer price changes on the quantities of all alcoholic drinks consumed are taken into account. For example, to the extent that the quantity of wine or spirits consumed responds to the change in beer prices, the model encompasses the consequent tax revenue changes from all beverages.

Additional features of the model and detailed results are given in the appendix. But the following summary is instructive. As illustrated in figure 2A, we have allowed the producer's supply price of beer to fall

---

29 A "cross price elasticity" shows how the demand for a commodity varies with the price of some other commodity. For example, a cross price elasticity of wine with respect to the price of spirits of 0.44 implies that a 1 percent increase in the price of spirits will result in a 0.44 percent increase in the demand for wine. The "own price elasticity" of demand for beer of -0.4 implies that a 1 percent increase in the price of beer will lead to a 0.4 percent decrease in the quantity of beer demanded. An elasticity with an absolute value less than unity is referred to as inelastic. A price fall for an inelastically demanded good will result in a fall in total expenditures due to the relatively unresponsive nature of output demanded to the price change.

by 10 percent (from P_s to P_s'). This translates into a similar, though not identical, fall in price to the consumer: P_c falls to P_c'. Thus, the equilibrium quantity of beer sold increases from q to q′ at corresponding prices. Total expenditure changes from $P_c aq0$ to $P_c'eq'0$ and total government revenue changes from $P_c abP_s$ to $P_c'efP_s'$.

In figure 2B we illustrate what happens in the spirits market. Given the particular set of elasticities in the model, the demand for spirits increases in response to a fall in the price of beer: i.e. D shifts to D′. Thus, there is an increase in expenditure on spirits from $P_c kq0$ to $P_c lq'0$ and this generates an increase in revenue both to the producer (of $stq'q$) and governments (of $klts$). Similar secondary effects are experienced in the wine industry.

The GIRAB-CAN model predicts that, in response to this 10 percent reduction in producer price, the provincial government sees a small increase in its overall revenue. The federal government also sees a small, yet slightly greater, increase than the provincial government. The reason for this disparity is that federal levies on beverages tend to have a higher specific than *ad valorem* tax content relative to the provincial government.[30] In particular, in the beer category, the increase in domestic sales yields virtually no overall revenue change for the federal government because the resulting revenue increase from excise duties (a specific levy) roughly balances its losses in GST revenue (an *ad valorem* levy). Both the provincial markups on beer and provincial sales taxes are *ad valorem*. Thus, the lower producer price shrinks this tax base, despite an increase in quantity consumed, because of the less than unit elastic demand for domestic beer. It is important to note that much of the increase in tax revenue results from a rise in the quantities consumed of wine and, particularly, spirits. The producers of domestic beer suffer a fall in revenues due to the inelastic demand for its product. However, if this is accompanied by a fall in production costs, it may not reflect a deterioration in profitability.

---

30 A specific tax is usually stated as a specific charge, say $.10, per unit of output. An *ad valorem* tax is a percentage of the value of a product. Note that as the price of a product rises the specific tax per unit of the commodity remains constant. The *ad valorem* tax, on the other hand, rises.

Figure 2a: The Market for Beer

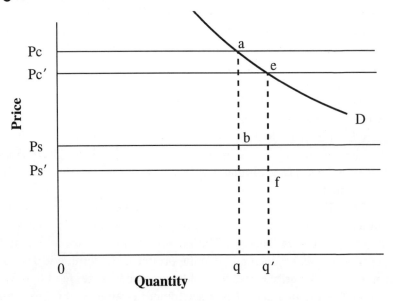

Figure 2b: The Market for Spirits

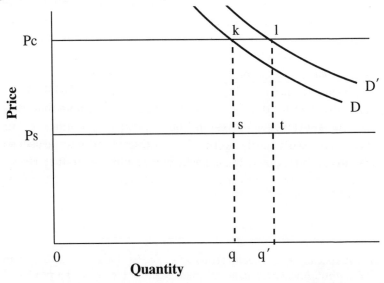

What does trade liberalization really mean?

Irvine *et al* (1990) emphasise the importance of *international* free trade as an element that would impose discipline on the domestic market. However, with the present high degree of concentration, the existing system of distribution and sales, minimum pricing laws in certain provinces, and other non price barriers to competition, a major reorganization of the industry may result in very limited benefit to most consumers. Without wider distributional access to the Canadian market, and freedom from strict minimum pricing laws, the potential for competition to exert pressure on the pricing of domestic beer will be severely circumscribed. In this section we develop these ideas and argue that there is much more to freeing up the beer industry in Canada than merely abolishing barriers to the shipment of beer between provinces.

Distribution and sales

Beer in Canada is sold for off-premises consumption in basically three different ways: Some provinces permit beer sales in convenience stores or hotels (e.g. Quebec and British Columbia), others require that it be sold in government owned outlets, and elsewhere (e.g. Ontario) a near monopoly on its sale is given to the Big Two through the Brewer's Warehousing Company.

In those provinces where the distribution of beer is not controlled by domestic producers, and where minimum pricing is not operative, the benefits to the consumer of a reduction in interprovincial and international barriers will be greater. In contrast, in provinces where minimum pricing exists (currently British Columbia, Ontario, Quebec, New Brunswick and Newfoundland), or where non- price barriers to market entry remain, consumers will share less in the gains from the removal of the production location barriers. While minimum pricing laws may prevent predatory pricing,[31] and thus help to insure a com-

---

31　It is usually assumed that the international dumping of a product is an example of such predatory pricing. In 1991 three American brewers (the Heileman Brewing Co. Ltd., the Stroh Brewing Co. and the Pabst Brewing Co.) were found to have dumped in B.C. (i.e. essentially selling their

petitive environment,[32] to the extent that they serve to maintain high prices and, equally importantly, to minimize the difference between the prices of Canadian and U.S. produced beer, the consumer will benefit correspondingly less. The current restrictions against firms, other than the Big Two, marketing directly to the public in provinces like Ontario then become less relevant. Space does not permit us to examine the regulations which exist in each province, but it is instructive to look at Ontario and Quebec, not only because they are the two biggest markets, but because these two markets function in very different ways.

Ontario

Since Ontario (a) accounts for almost 40 percent of total Canadian consumption, (b) is believed to account for two thirds of Labatt and Molson profits (De Verteuil, 1992) and (c) has restrictive distribution practices, it merits special attention. The profitability stems in part from low costs associated with the centralized Brewer's Retail distribution system. It is not surprising therefore that the environmental levy and the new Ontario service charge on imported beer favour domestic bottled beer over the imported U.S. canned product. These new levies, which have increased the relative price of an imported 6-pack of cans

---

product in Canada at a price below that which they were charging in the U.S.). But predatory pricing involves selling a product *below cost* in order to monopolize a market. It is not clear that this beer was being sold below cost. Indeed Heilman argued that the brand of beer (Rainier) that it allegedly dumped is sold as a premium beer in Washington state, due to name recognition, but as a discount beer not only in B.C., but also in states adjacent to Washington. If anything, the behaviour by these breweries is an example of discriminatory pricing. Interestingly it was Heileman and Stroh that, in 1990, complained to U.S. trade authorities about unfair Canadian marketing practices with regard to imported beer. This complaint ultimately lead to a GATT ruling against Canada in 1991.

32   Some authors argue that predatory pricing may not be the most effective way to monopolize a market (McGee, 1958). In any case, an extremely high degree of concentration in the Canadian market is a *fait accompli*. The most likely rationale for minimum price regulation is therefore either to insulate the industry from price competition or to protect the Canadian consumer from low beer prices! For more on the modern view of predatory pricing see Ordover and Saloner, 1989.

by $.75 (De Verteuil, 1992), have solidified the Big Two's position in this market.[33]

To see the importance of the Brewer's Warehousing System, imagine for a moment that the market for snowsuits in Ontario were dominated by two firms, and that over 90 percent of the market was supplied by them. Further, assume that the provincial government decreed that these two firms could form a marketing chain which would have almost sole rights to distribute, not just their own snowsuits, but the snowsuits of other domestic and foreign producers. Suppose now that the various levels of government in Canada implemented "free trade" by reducing levies and punitive tariffs on imported and out-of-province products, but left the retailing system untouched, and contentedly told themselves that the interests of the snowsuit buying public were well served by such policies. To stretch the imagination a little further, say there were two additional elements to the story: first, that the monopoly distributor (owned by the two big companies) then proposed to the government and its competition that *it* would act as a public benefactor by agreeing to market the competing snowsuits with all due care and attention and second, that the government decreed there would be a minimum price at which any manufacturer could sell their snowsuits.

This indeed seems like an Alice in Wonderland story. But, *grosso modo*, it describes the retailing of beer in Ontario. This has prompted

---

33 The new charges involve a service charge on imports, which is designed to bring the cost of imported beer more in line with the distribution costs incurred by the Liquor Control Board of Ontario (L.C.B.O.) in shipping the good to various locations. The second charge involves a $.10 environmental charge on non-refillable containers. Similar environmental charges are being considered in B.C. and Quebec. It is not surprising, given the importance of this market to Canadian brewing, that such charges were first implemented in Ontario.

In response to these charges the U.S. has recently imposed a retaliatory duty on all beer imports from Ontario. The Canadian government has reacted to this with its own set of increased duties on products produced by the Heileman and Stroh breweries and imported into Ontario. These are 2 of the 3 breweries which were found to have been "dumping" beer in B.C. in 1991 and it was these 2 breweries whose complaints in 1990 led to a GATT ruling against Canada for unfair treatment of imported beer.

several observers to question the appropriateness of the system. For example, McKinnon (1992) states

> Ontario is the only jurisdiction in the world in which the largest brewers control beer retailing. Through Brewer's Retail, Molson and Labatt dictate the terms of retail policy to their smaller competitors. Recently, with cavalier disregard for the consumer, Brewers Retail shut down 39 of its outlets, forcing many Ontarians to take half hour car trips . . . just to buy beer.

The right to distribute in outlets other than those owned by one's competitors is an essential element in any successful effort to inject competition into the industry. Quite apart from pricing policies, the ability to insure a reliable supply of one's own product, plus the ability to establish one's own brand image, are essential ingredients in competition, more widely defined.[34]

Frequently the argument is made that the sale of bulky goods such as beer is most efficiently carried out in centralised locations, and hence convenience store sales are not efficient because of their higher distribution costs. Whatever the merits of this argument, it is not an argument for monopoly distribution rights, only an argument for centralized distribution.[35]

---

34   An example will help to illustrate our point here. Recently, Moosehead, which is brewed in the Maritimes, gained access to the Ontario market. The ordering policy of the LCBO is based upon the *average* stock of beer in the Province as a whole. At a certain point it was noted that Moosehead was selling much better in Toronto and Ottawa than in other locations and that at times no Moosehead was available at these specific points of sale, while a surplus was available at other locations. However, the outlets demanding the product were not necessarily restocked because the *average* stock of Moosehead had not reached the threshold level. The resolution to this problem was that Moosehead was ultimately given the right to undertake the transport of beer between outlets within the province!

35   It should be noted that a reasonable social policy is to set limits on the availability of alcoholic beverages. The Addiction Research Foundation (ARF) is a proponent of such views (e.g. Ferris and Room, 1992). The views expressed above do not necessarily conflict with such policies. An example of a competitive mode which would be consistent with the goals of the ARF would be one where a competing chain of retailers, subject to the same general regulations as Brewers Retail, would have freedom to market beer

In addition to the restrictions on market accessibility, producers from outside Ontario must incur shipping costs in excess of those incurred by Molson and Labatt. By using its power deriving from the *Importation of Intoxicating Liquors Act*—specifically, the "right of first receivership" provision, Ontario requires out-of-province firms to deliver their beer to a specific warehouse of the *Liquor Control Board of Ontario* (LCBO). From there it is shipped to the stores owned by the LCBO or to the Brewers Retail outlets. This is a cost which need not be incurred by firms located within the province. It appears that the principal motivation for maintaining this regulation is to protect the brewers located in Ontario.

An obvious question to ask at this point is why foreign firms could not just set up production in Ontario. There are several reasons why this is unlikely. First, they would have to operate at a small scale of production and thus lose the cost advantage which they may have if they produced beer from their current U.S. plants. Second, and very important, is the minimum pricing law in Ontario. This law essentially insures that the price difference between domestic and foreign beer can be kept at a minimum. If the Canadian consumer views the domestic beer as being superior to U.S. beer, he or she is unlikely to demand the latter unless it is offered at a substantial price discount. The minimum pricing law would therefore prevent a U.S. entrant from gaining a significant market share. Third, there exist franchise agreements between the Big Two and certain U.S. producers which would limit both the profitability and the feasibility of this.[36]

The most recent development in Ontario has been the conclusion of an agreement between Canada and the U.S. in August 1993, which effectively ended the 1992/93 Ontario-U.S. "beer war." The main components of this agreement were: i) a lifting of the punitive levies which had been imposed by each side on the other's beer exports; ii) a lowering

---

(e.g. the new microbrewers retailing in concert with foreign or specialty brewers).

36 The franchise agreements are between Canada's Big Two and *specific* American brewers (e.g. Miller and A.B.). If a U.S. brewer were to set up in Ontario it would therefore more likely be one of the mid-sized brewers.

of the minimum price for beer in Ontario, by between one and two dollars per case of 24 depending upon alcohol content; iii) greater accessibility to Ontario customers for U.S. brewers via the Brewer's Retail outlets; iv) the maintenance of the environmental levy on cans.

This agreement is significant in that it permits the consumer to share in the benefits of rationalization and the lowering of interprovincial barriers. However, given the ability of governments to set tax rates on alcohol, a minimum price serves no obvious purpose other than to protect domestic producers. In addition, under present rules, 3 percent alcohol beer sells for almost the same price as 7 percent alcohol beer. It makes no sense that consumers should not be free to purchase the former at a significantly lower price than the latter. But minimum pricing has effectively ruled this out. Furthermore, this agreement has put the potential competition (mainly the U.S. brewers) into a straight-jacket, making price competition unlikely for the foreseeable future. Lastly, it leaves the control of sales and distribution in the hands of the two major domestic producers.

Quebec

While it is Ontario which is frequently portrayed as the villain in restrictive practices, the market in the second biggest province (Quebec) is also characterised by a number of regulations which effectively inhibit the entry of foreign competition. In Quebec beer is sold either in stores owned by the government through the Societe des Alcools du Quebec (SAQ), or in private retail outlets (convenience stores, restaurants, bars etc.). In June 1992, *Bill 6* was enacted. This modified the SAQ act, which, *inter alia*, governs the distribution of alcoholic beverages in Quebec. From the standpoint of competition what is important in this act is the differential treatment it affords producers located in different areas.

Brewers located in Quebec are allowed to distribute their beer directly to the various points of sale (convenience stores, etc) or to use another party for this purpose; that is "a brewer's permit authorizes the holder to carry on any operation authorized under a beer distributor's permit" (*Bill 6*, section 3).

Brewers *located outside Quebec*, in order to distribute their beer, must acquire a *distributor's* permit. However, under *Bill 6* (section 4) such a permit only authorizes the holder to sell and deliver beer that is "made by the holder or by a corporation related to the holder." Furthermore, the conditions defining how corporations are related are made very explicit. Bill 6 essentially requires that the distributor be an almost wholly owned subsidiary of the producer or vice versa, and that the distributor be located in Quebec.

The implications are that a non-Quebec brewer must set up an operating corporate entity in Quebec in order to sell beer in the Province. Such a requirement operates against the basic principles of trade and specialization and acts as a very effective barrier to entry. This is not because a potential competitor is *legally* prevented from setting up a business. Rather, to break into the market, the foreign competitor would suffer from having to own and operate a distribution system of suboptimal size.[37] But it is really the combination of this regulation with two further stipulations, to which we now turn, that makes the cost of doing business in Quebec for foreign competitors higher than for Quebec firms.

The first of these is that beer produced outside the province must generally be shipped to a SAQ warehouse, where it can be tested, checked for labelling, etc. before it can be shipped to the distributor and sold to retailers. Thus, a brewer located in the U.S. would have to incur two extra distribution costs not incurred by a Quebec brewer: the cost of delivering his beer to a SAQ establishment and then the cost of retrieving it. We note that there is nothing very unusual about an arrangement whereby the beer must be shipped to the SAQ initially - similar procedures exist in other provinces. However, from the standpoint of the consumer, this places an additional transportation cost on a set of suppliers and accordingly reduces the potential for competitive pricing.

In the course of recent discussions between the provinces and the federal government, proposals have been examined which would enable *Canadian* brewed beer from outside Quebec to be shipped directly

---

37 To avoid the suboptimal size problem, the foreign producer could own/purchase an existing distribution company—for example, one that distributes other goods to convenience stores. At the time of writing, the limits of such possibilities were being tested at a hearing involving Lakeport Brewers of Hamilton, Ontario.

to the distributor in Quebec without first going to the SAQ. This would appear to be an integral part of the dismantling of the interprovincial trade barriers. But, equally, it limits competition to a very small number of players. Foreign beer would still go through the SAQ system, rather than directly to a distributor or agent. One must infer that such an agreement would not be in conflict with GATT regulations.

The other impediment to the entry of foreign competition is the Quebec regulations dealing with beer containers. Sales in convenience stores etc., in order to avoid penalty, must be in refillable containers. Specifically, if more than one third of Quebec sales for a producer (regardless of point of production) are in the form of non-refillable containers, a penalty is imposed on the sales above the threshold allowed. This charge is in addition to the standard deposit on bottles and cans. *De facto* this constitutes a barrier to many foreign producers, who produce almost solely in cans.

In summary, despite the easing of certain trade barriers there are still substantial distributional obstacles faced by foreign brewers not faced by domestic ones. These include first having to ship their beer to the SAQ warehouse before being able to deliver it to retail outlets; second, having to set up operating corporate entities which would not be able to take advantage of the returns to scale which characterise the operation of warehousing and distribution; and third, being subject to penalties depending on the containers they use. Thus, the cost of doing business in the "post barrier" era will not be significantly reduced from what it has been in the past for foreign brewers, but it may be considerably less for big domestic brewers.

What can one infer about the regulation process from this? One view is that the big brewers have been successful in maintaining a set of barriers to effective competition. Another is that the ethos of the regulating body has a life of its own: the regulating body wishes to see its own function assume a continued importance and/or it wishes to protect the interests of Canadian and Quebec based brewers, even if this means unnecessary costs to the consumer.

Despite the institutional barriers to trade in Quebec, the Quebec government introduced a minimum pricing policy in November 1993. This means that almost 70 percent of Canadian consumers are now facing minimum pricing.

Transportation, packaging and brands

The cost studies which have been undertaken for the Canadian brewing industry indicate that minimum efficient scale lies in the two to three million hectolitre range. Why then do we observe the newest breweries in the U.S. with capacities in the range of ten to twenty million hectolitres? There are several reasons for this. First there are major differences in the transportation systems, related to the density of the market, trucking costs and the use of cans rather than returnable bottles. Shipping costs are significantly lower in the U.S. than in Canada because of the lower price of gasoline, and a less regulated trucking industry. In conjunction with much greater population densities, this means that the major brewers can build larger breweries and take advantage of the scale economies up to much higher production levels. While the increasing returns to scale may decline after three million hectolitres, they are clearly significant enough to promote the construction of plant with several times that capacity. The density of adjoining populations further makes it profitable to set up satellite canning/bottling plants to which the beer is shipped in bulk from the mega breweries.[38]

In Canada, in contrast, shipping costs are higher due to higher costs in the trucking industry and to the requirement that beer be shipped in returnable bottles. However, if it were the case that sufficiently large populations existed in adjoining locations it might still be profitable for Canadian firms to adopt a pattern of centralized production and satellite bottling/canning. This pattern is evolving in certain areas of Canada, as evidenced by the recent decision of Canadian National Railway (CN) to purchase tank cars for bulk beer shipping (Brewers Association of Canada, 1992). Indeed, at the present time, Miller Genuine Draft is shipped in bulk from British Columbia to Ontario, where it is bottled and sold. However, the Canadian industry is unlikely to move to the U.S. scale of production and bulk shipping in the foreseeable future,

---

38 For example, Coors, which supplies about 10 percent of the U.S. market from its single plant in Colorado, ships in bulk for canning to Virginia—a distance of almost 3,000 kilometres. This beer is then distributed to the eastern seaboard states.

because of the distances, population densities and the use of returnable bottles.

But the required use of returnable bottles ultimately begs the important question of why this form of packaging should continue. First, with plants moving to a larger scale, canning could become more cost efficient than bottling, purely from a packaging standpoint. The pattern observed in the U.S. in recent decades is evidence of this. Second, the shipment of beer in cans is less costly than in bottles, both because cans are lighter and are of a more efficient physical form. Third, the cost associated with the return shipment of cans (which can as easily be subject to a deposit as bottles) is significantly less.

In view of this, one must ask why the industry and governments continue to favour bottles, particularly since the soft drink industry in Canada is rapidly switching away from glass towards cans and plastic containers. In Ontario for example, the ratio of soft drink cans to beer cans may be on the order of one hundred to one. Yet it is only this minuscule fraction of the market which is subject to an environmental levy! Thus, just as with the distributional barriers analyzed earlier, it is difficult not to conclude that the real reason for the maintenance of bottles is not environmental, but to protect domestic producers from U.S. competition, since virtually all beer imported from the U.S. is in cans.

A second important distinction between the U.S. and Canadian production structures is the multitude of brands/labels produced by each of the major brewers in Canada. In contrast, the U.S. producers concentrate upon a very small number of brands. Elzinga (1990) emphasises that this has been a major factor in Anheuser-Busch's performance in the U.S. market in the last two decades

> All of its breweries are large, low cost facilities. . . . Moreover, much of the output takes the form of only one brand, produced primarily in one package format. . . . This means Anheuser-Busch does not often incur the cost of changing brewing formulas or reconstituting packaging lines. Anheuser-Busch's pricing strategy builds on the firm's efficiencies in production.

With fewer brands and greater production volumes firms can benefit fully from the returns to scale that a large production facility affords. Furthermore, "down" time and "scrubbing" costs at the plant are minimized by having fewer large batches. Historically, Canadian producers have produced a greater variety of products than their U.S. counterparts. McCafferty and McCullogh (1982) point out that as many as 20 different labels were sold in Ontario by Carling-O'Keefe in the early eighties. While this is far above the norm, the Big Three produced about 70 different labels nationally at this time, with production in each province being a subset of this larger number. While the production of a subset of the brands in each province certainly reduces production costs, maintaining a long menu of labels nationwide affords the producer little opportunity to benefit from the returns to scale associated with national advertising.

The multitude of labels produced by the Big Two springs in large part from the fact that these brewers grew to their current prominence by taking over small brewers. These latter generally had high local consumer loyalty to their brands. Thus, maintaining a long menu of labels for the major firms was seen as a way of maintaining their market share. This was therefore quite a different process from what has been observed in some other sectors, where dominant producers have sought to prevent entry by potential competitors, through multiplying their products.

Brand proliferation is intimately linked with both advertising and marketing costs. With more price competition in the industry the major producers would likely be forced to reduce their brand numbers in favour of a much leaner production structure. The present brand proliferation is far from optimal either for the consumer or for the producer. It increases production costs and prices for the benefit of very minimal differences in products. But the consuming market could be as well served by a reduced menu of products from the major producers (particularly when the product differences are so small) at a reduced price, and some additional products from foreign producers and specialty domestic brewers. Indeed, there is evidence for the Canadian manufacturing sector which indicates that tariff reduction has led to a decline in plant product diversity and to a corresponding increase in specialization (Baldwin and Gorecki, 1986).

Despite the decision by the Big Two to eliminate certain brands during the most post merger era, developments in the market place in the last year have seen them proliferate. In part, this has been due to a growth in market share by micro brewers, but in particular by Lakeport Brewing, which claimed 4 percent of the Ontario market in 1992/93. Lakeport uses the *President's Choice* label, under franchise, and established its market share by underpricing the Big Two. In conjunction with preparing for the entry of U.S. beer on a wider scale, the Big Two responded with "no image" beer at a comparable price and also high alcohol, premium-priced products in an effort to maintain overall profitability.

This reproliferation on the part of the Big Two will reduce cost competitiveness in the industry. Ironically, the short term effects of minimum pricing may be to preserve a degree of competition—i.e., the survival of Lakeport. The enormous concentration in the industry would otherwise enable the Big Two to price compete using their no image brands, yet maintain profitability overall through their image brands, and force their competition out of the market. This problem of "cross subsidization" is a classic one for multi-product firms. Yet it should be emphasized that the main reason such a strategy would be feasible is that the incumbent firms are highly insulated from foreign competition. If premium U.S. beers could sell freely in the market, the possibility of such predatory practices would be severely limited.

Advertising

Consumers are subject to extensive advertising from brewers in a wide variety of forms. Advertising and marketing expenditures per hectolitre for the major brewing companies in Canada are at about twice the level of their U.S. counterparts. The major Canadian brewers engage in non-price competition over market share, and it is questionable whether this provides benefits to either the firms or the consuming public.

Economists might view this situation as a type of "prisoner's dilemma," in that each of the firms would benefit if both cut back their advertising and promotional expenditures, but there is an incentive for each to renege on such an agreement. However, freer all round trade may bring with it the benefits of reduced advertising and fewer labels, leading to lower producer costs and reduced consumer prices.

At present, the Canadian brewers present a picture of advertising as one which serves to increase market share rather than affect the total sales of the industry. Furthermore, since this advertising tends to be "lifestyle" rather than informative, neither producers nor consumers would suffer from its reduction, if its effect on total sales is minimal. However, if it becomes necessary to compete on a *price* basis producers may not be able to afford the current extensive levels of advertising. As a corollary the current high advertising expenditures may be due to limited price competition.[39]

Rationalization, efficiencies and pricing

Throughout this essay we have argued that two factors have been paramount in improving industry efficiency: the removal of interprovincial barriers to trade and the prospect of competition. In view of our discussions in the preceding section, the prospect of serious price competition in a large segment of the national industry seems remote. However, it may be argued that the *threat* of competition has made a significant contribution to resource allocation: the failure of strong price competition to materialize means only that it is the *distribution* of the gains which is at issue—if the consumer gains little and the producer a lot, the industry is still enormously more efficient. This view, however, is not correct since it overlooks the additional welfare gains which could accrue from the actual introduction of price competition. We explore these gains with the help of Figure 3.

As before, we denote the consumer and producer prices by P_c and P_s respectively, and demand by D. The difference between P_s and unit cost (AC) is a profit markup. Let the initial quantity consumed be q and the margin between the producer and consumer price consist of taxes and other government levies. AC and AC' represent unit costs at this output before and after rationalization respectively. MC' is the marginal cost of production post rationalization. The value of the efficiency gains is therefore q (AC - AC') which all goes to the producer if the price

---

39 An alternative interpretation of image advertising is that producers bundle it with their product, and it is the combination of advertising and the good which provide utility. In these circumstances, a reduction in advertising could reduce utility.

Figure 3: The Market for Beer in Canada

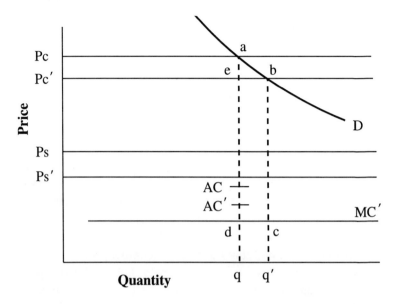

remains unchanged. Resource gains have thus materialised and are substantial.

However, if rationalization is accompanied by price competition the consumer price can be expected to fall, say from P_c to P_c' in Figure 3. This will not simply effect a transfer of some of this gain, but will generate further resource gains, through an increase in output, since the price of the product exceeds its marginal cost. A basic proposition in welfare economics is that when price is in excess of marginal cost an increase in output increases welfare, since the value which consumers place on the product (represented by the price they pay) is greater than the cost of producing it. Conversely, a reduction in output would reduce economic welfare in this situation. While the demand for beer is price inelastic, and such increases in output will therefore be limited, the additional gains may still be substantial. This is because the gains are not only inversely related to demand elasticities, but are directly related to the size of the wedge between price and marginal cost. In this instance, as discussed in section 1, that wedge is very high—with the tax component accounting, typically, for about half of the consumer price. Furthermore, the difference between producer price and marginal cost is substantial for small changes in output.[40] The welfare gain associated with a price decline from P_c to P_c' is given by the area *abcd*: the difference between the consumers' willingness to pay for additional units of output beyond q, and their production cost. It is simple to calculate the approximate value of such a change: if the demand elasticity is assumed to be -0.5, a 10 percent decline in consumer price will increase quantity sold by 5 percent. If the marginal cost is one quarter of consumer price then the area *abcd* amounts to approximately 3.5 percent of expenditure on beer.[41] While this is less than the value of the efficiency gains, by any customary standard in welfare economics it represents a significant gain in resource allocation.[42]

Conclusion[43]

In concluding, we emphasise several points which we have developed in detail in the main body of the paper and which have received insufficient attention in public debate.

---

40 In particular, advertising and marketing are non-production related and even much of distribution costs would be unchanged in response to a small increase in output.

41 We note that, if part of the tax wedge represents a corrective element for the externalities associated with alcohol consumption the true social gain would be less than the 3.5 percent figure. The role of the tax wedge as a corrective element is discussed in some detail in Irvine and Sims (1993a).

42 An important aspect of the above analysis is that it examines only the market for domestic beer. The analysis becomes somewhat more complex if we introduce the concept of competition in the marketplace between domestically produced and imported beer. The same general conclusions are likely to hold in such a scenario. The details of the analysis are worked out in Irvine and Sims (1993b).

43 In this paper, discussion of barriers and regulations in the U.S. which may hinder the export of Canadian beer has been minimal. The analysis has focused upon Canada for the simple reason that Canadian barriers are the subject of this essay. No doubt a more complete picture of the beer market would emerge if space permitted us to undertake an examination of U.S. regulations. But the fact that we omit this does not imply that Canadian

First, it is widely recognised that both the Molson-Carling merger and the removal of interprovincial barriers to the shipment of beer will increase the industry's efficiency enormously. However, further major efficiency gains, some of which are already underway, are to be reaped through the standardization of bottles, the reduction in marketing and advertising costs and a smaller product line. *Competition is an essential ingredient in this process.* Accordingly, laws and regulations which place unfair bounds on the competitive process will reduce the extent and likelihood of such gains.

Our second point, developed in section 6, is that while the threat of competition has served the industry well up to the present time—by speeding along cost reducing measures—actual price competition, by inducing price reductions, would likely generate further gains in the market because of the excess of price over marginal cost. However, *reform has failed to eliminate the regulations in some provinces that limit the potential for such competition.* We have illustrated the consequences of such regulations in Ontario and Quebec.

Finally, *interprovincial barriers will leave a legacy of high costs to the industry.* In a certain sense, what we observe in Ontario—a successful effort by the Big Two to restrict access to the marketplace by competitors—is a result of the interprovincial barriers. Despite the restructuring, the Canadian industry is a high cost industry relative to the U.S.—regardless of the scale of production. This higher cost stems from the fact that, historically, the industry has been insulated from international competition. With Ontario responsible for such a high proportion of industry profits, and being saddled with high costs, it would appear that the producers and successive governments have cooperated to maintain minimum pricing and to grant the Big Two a near monopoly on distribution. The point to be stressed here is that the Ontario marketing structure is an outcome of poor provincial government policy: had interprovincial barriers not been in place and had punitive levies on imports not been imposed, the industry would not have found itself with its present high cost structure and the attendant need to control sales, as it is currently doing successfully.

---

brewers have free and unencumbered access to U.S. markets.

References

Anastasopoulos, A., I. J. Irvine and W. A. Sims (1986). *Free Trade Between Canada and the United States in Alcoholic Beverages*, Institute of Applied Economic Research, Concordia University.

Baldwin, J. and P. Gorecki (1986). "The Relationship between plant scale and product diversity in Canadian Manufacturing industries" *Journal of Industrial Economics* 24, 373-88.

Berndt, E. R. and D. M. Hesse (1986). "Measuring and Assessing Capacity Utilization in the Manufacturing Sectors of Nine OECD Countries" *European Economic Review* 30, 961-89.

Boadway, R. W. and N. Bruce (1984). *Welfare Economics* (Basil Blackwell Publishers Ltd.)

Brewers Association of Canada (1986). *On Tap*, July.

Brewers Association of Canada (1987). *On Tap*, July.

Brewers Association of Canada (1990). *The Brewing Industry in Canada in 1990*, Ottawa.

Brewers Association of Canada (1991). *Alcoholic Beverage Taxation and Control Policies*.

Brewers Association of Canada (1992). *On Tap*, November.

Brewers Association of Canada (1993). *On Tap*, March.

Brophy, M. (1993) *Streamlined Brewing and Entertainment Company Expected to Yield 34 percent Total Return Over Next 18 Months*, First Boston, September 21.

Conference Board of Canada (1990). *An Assessment of the Impacts of Liberalised Interprovincial Trade in Canada*, Ottawa.

De Verteuil, I. (1992). *Brewing Update*, Burns-Fry, July 3.

Elzinga, K. G. (1990). "The Beer Industry" in W. Adams (ed.) *The Structure of American Industry* (MacMillan Publishing Co.).

Ferris, J. and R. Room, (1992). "Opinions on Alcohol and Tobacco Policies, Ontario 1992" Addiction Research Foundation, Toronto, Ontario.

FOCUS (1988). *GATT Newsletter*, April/May, vol. 54.

FOCUS (1992). *GATT Newsletter*, March, vol. 54.

Goldberg, M. A. and C. C. Eckel (1983). *Price Competition in the British Columbia Brewing Industry: Present Status and Future Prospects*, A Report for the Minister of Consumer and Corporate Affairs, Government of British Columbia.

Gorman, W. M. (1959). "Separable Utility and Aggregation" *Econometrica* 27, 469-481.

Irvine, I. J., W. A. Sims and A. Anastasopoulos (1990). "Interprovincial Versus International Free Trade in the Brewing Industry" *Canadian Journal of Economics* 23, 332-47.

Irvine, I. J. and W. A. Sims (1991). "GIRAB-CAN: A Disaggregated Computer Simulation Model of Alcoholic Beverage Demand in Canada" Department of Economics Discussion Paper 9101, Concordia University: Montreal.

Irvine, I. J. and W. A. Sims (1992). "The consumption of alcoholic beverages and Laffer effects" Department of Economics, Concordia University, Montreal, working paper.

Irvine, I. J. and W. A. Sims (1993a). "The welfare effects of alcohol taxation" forthcoming, *The Journal of Public Economics*.

Irvine, I. J. and W.A. Sims (1993b). "Interprovincial barriers to beer trade in Canada" Department of Economics, Concordia University, Montreal, working paper.

Jones, J. C. H. (1967). "Mergers and Competition: The Brewing Case" *Canadian Journal of Economics and Political Science* 33, 551-68.

Leibenstein, H. (1966). "Allocative Efficiency vs. 'X-inefficiency'" *American Economic Review* 56, 392-415.

Lomas, B. (1992). *John Labatt Limited (LBT): Greater Value Still to Emerge from Labatt*, Scotia-McLeod, October 5.

McCafferty, R. and F. McCullough (1982). *Canadian Brewing Industry - Industry Review*, Dominion Securities Ames.

McGee, J. (1958). "Predatory price cutting: The Standard Oil (N.J.) Case" *Journal of Law and Economics* 1, 137-69.

McKinnon, J. (1992). "Ontario the Villain in Beer Battle" *Globe and Mail*, July 30.

Ordover, J. A. and G. Saloner (1989). "Predation, Monopolization and Antitrust" in R. Schmalensee and R. D. Willig (eds.) *Handbook of Industrial Organization* Volume 1 (Elsevier Science Publishers).

Sfiligoj, E. (1992). "Top 10 Beers: Rank and Market Size" *Beverage Industry*, January, 14-17.

Smith, J. B. and W. A. Sims (1985). "The impact of pollution charges on productivity growth in Canadian brewing" *Rand Journal of Economics* 16, 410- 423.

Strotz, R. H. (1957). "The empirical implications of a utility tree" *Econometrica* 25, 269-80.

Tsiritakis, M., Campbell, C. and A. Merikas (1990). "The cost of scale inefficiency in the Canadian brewing industry: a multi product cost function approach" *The Journal of Applied Business Research* 7, 16-24.

Wolf, A. (1991). "Beer Seer" *Beverage World*, December, 20-26.

Appendix 1

The theory underlying GIRAB-CAN is described in detail in Irvine and Sims (1991). The behavioral model is based on the utility tree approach first suggested by Strotz (1957) and Gorman (1959). A representative consumer is assumed to allocate a budget between alcoholic beverages and all other goods. This allocation depends only on the prices of these two aggregates and the consumer's tastes. Once overall expenditures on alcohol are determined, purchases of beer, wine and spirits then result from maximizing a subutility function for alcoholic beverages, subject to relative prices. Finally, the expenditures within each beverage group are determined in accordance with a further subutility function for each beverage. Data in the model are for 1989 but have been updated to account for the replacement of the federal sales tax (FST) with the goods and services tax (GST) in 1991. The supply side of the model is straightforward: producers mark up their production costs to yield a selling price, which is then subject to a series of levies by the federal and provincial governments to yield a consumer price.

We have simulated the model for the province of Ontario by assuming that the price of domestically brewed beer could fall by 10 percent in a "rationalized" world. The precise value we use is not important, since the results will be qualitatively the same for greater or smaller price increases.

A key feature of the model is that it has a matrix of cross price elasticities embedded within it. This means that the effects of price changes on the quantities consumed of all alcoholic drinks can be traced: when the price of any single good changes, new price indices are calculated at each level of aggregation and the expenditure responses to such changes are calculated. This means that the responsiveness of the spirits and wine categories and the changes in industry and government revenues which follow are calculable. These changes are detailed in table A1.

The first column in the table defines the percentage change in consumer price due to a 10 percent reduction in domestic producer prices. Column two gives the percentage changes in quantities consumed in response to these price changes. (These resemble cross price elasticities, however, three prices are changed rather than one to obtain the effects). The cross elasticities can be high in GIRAB-CAN for reasons discussed in Irvine and Sims (1992). Columns 3, 4, and 5 define the percentage changes in revenues to the provincial government, producers and the federal government respectively. Table A2 presents the elasticities of demand embedded in GIRAB-CAN.

We note first that a producer price reduction of 10 percent results in a less than 10 percent reduction in consumer price. This is because some of the government levies are specific rather than *ad valorem*. Such a price reduction results in the predictable pattern of quantity changes within the beer category: imports fall while domestic beers increase. We note also an increase in the quantities of spirits and wine consumed. This arises because, since beer is inelastically demanded, a reduction in its price means a fall in total beer expenditure which is greater than the overall reduction in expenditure on alcoholic beverages. Thus expenditures on the other two beverages rise.

The model has also been simulated subject to a different set of elasticities, since there is no universal agreement on the appropriate magnitudes for these estimates. The broad pattern of results is similar while the magnitudes differ in a predictable manner.

Table A2: Price Elasticity Matrix Implicit in Table A1*

Price Quantity	Beer	Wine	Spirits
Beer	−.40	.04	.12
Wine	−.43	−.85	.44
Spirits	−.48	.16	−.61

* Assumed elasticity of demand for alcohol = −.55.

Table A1: Simulated Effects of Domestic Beer Producer Price Reductions of 10%

	%ΔP	%ΔQ	%ΔPGR	%ΔPR	%ΔFGR
Spirits					
Dom.Whiskey	.0000	.035	.035	.035	.035
Dom. White	.0000	.035	.035	.035	.035
Dom. Liqueurs	.0000	.035	.035	.035	.035
Dom. Rum	.0000	.035	.035	.035	.035
Imp. Whiskey	.0000	.035	.035	.035	.035
Imp. White	.0000	.035	.035	.035	.035
Imp. Liqueurs	.0000	.035	.035	.035	.035
Imp. Rums	.0000	.035	.035	.035	.035
Coolers	.0000	.035	.035	.035	.035
Wine	.0000	.0315	.0315	.0315	.0315
Dom. <7%	.0000	.0315	.0315	.0315	.0315
Dom. >7%	.0000	.0315	.0315	.0315	.0315
Imp. <7%	.0000	.0315	.0315	.0315	.0315
Imp. >7%	.0000	.0315	.0315	.0315	.0315
Beer					
Dom. Light	−.0782	.0354	−.0328	−.0682	.0058
Dom. Regular	−.0774	.0347	−.0325	−.0687	.0060
Dom. Premium	−.0817	.0385	−.0348	−.0653	.0040
Imp. Light	.0000	−.0300	−.0300	−.0300	−.0300
Imp. Regular	.0000	−.0300	−.0300	−.0300	−.0300
Imp. Premium	.0000	−.0300	−.0300	−.0300	−.0300
Total	**−.0172**	—	**.0095**	**−.0407**	**.0196**

The columns define the percentage changes in consumer price (ΔP), quantity purchased (ΔQ), provincial government revenues (ΔPGR), producer revenues (ΔPR) and federal government revenues (ΔFGR).

Financial Markets in Canada: Regulation in a Small Economy in Global Markets

John C. Pattison[1]

T HIS CHAPTER DISCUSSES THE MYSTERIES of financial regulation in Canada's complex federal-provincial structure. It attempts to describe the framework in which financial institutions are regulated in Canada and to point out the consequences for financial intermediation- the process of moving funds from those with surpluses to those who wish to borrow. These consequences affect the efficiency, costs and yields at which borrowers borrow and savers receive a yield on their

---

1   The author is a Senior Vice-President at the Canadian Imperial Bank of Commerce. However, this paper has been prepared in a personal capacity. The author alone bears full responsibility for its contents. Lisa Wark is thanked for her assistance with the production of this essay. Derek Hayes, Brian Quinlan and Leighton Reid have been kind enough to offer comments on an earlier draft.

investments as well as the ability to engage in intermediation across provincial boundaries. The consequence, of course, is interprovincial barriers to the movement of capital or the conduct of business. My task will be to elucidate how the Canadian financial regulatory system functions in our federal provincial structure, to point out the costs and implications and to suggest ways for improvement. It will be done by an analysis of the methods and tools of regulation as well as by case studies from a couple of financial industries. The complexity is great, but this seemingly remote constitutional and legal structure comes to have an effect on individual savers, investors and borrowers.

In pursuing this grail it will be useful to keep the international connections in mind. On the one hand financial markets are global and fiercely competitive. Money moves by electronic transfer from Tokyo to Regina or Quebec City to New York based upon minute differences in yields. As a consequence there are agreements among many of the governments on financial regulation. Sometimes these are straightforward, as in banking. Bank regulators meet regularly under the auspices of the Bank for International Settlements in Basle, Switzerland, and at the Organization for Economic Cooperation and Development in Paris. However, in the securities field no one speaks for Canada, as securities regulation is a provincial affair. As a result, agreements with foreign governments have been entered into by the securities commissions of Ontario, Quebec and sometimes British Columbia.

A second way of looking at the international experience is to draw on other experiences or models of financial regulation. An example is the European Community, currently with 12 member countries, which provides an interesting parallel to Canada, with 12 provinces and territories.[2] The goal of the European Community is to have a European financial market that has no barriers either to competition or to the free movement of funds among the member countries. Canada and its provinces have never agreed to such a comprehensive agreement as that which these sovereign nations are close to achieving. Canadian provin-

2   For an introduction see John C. Pattison, "Bank Marketing Strategies in the EC", Chapter 8 in John A. Quelch, Robert D. Buzzell and Eric Salama, *The Marketing Challenge of Europe 1992*, Reading, Massachusetts: Addison-Wesley Publishing Company, 1990.

cial trust and securities regulators regularly vaunt their success at harmonization as a result of regular meetings among regulators. However, this is harmonization to improve regulation, not to help consumers consume, or suppliers provide, more products at lower distribution costs.

It is important to realize that there are many players in this drama. In addition to the federal government and the twelve provinces and territories the other interest groups are not only savers, investors, borrowers and the hundreds of bank, trust, insurance, securities firms, credit unions and so forth, but also the regional manifestations of their political agendas. The governments are subject to pressures from many sides. Hence harmonization is going to be heavily constrained. Many interest groups oppose changes which increase competition, even though the consumer will have more choices and better prices. Others oppose change because they feel that more regulation will be the outcome.

Such harmonization as occurs is often only agreement on the lowest common denominator acceptable to the governments, not to consumers or the marketplace in general. Europe, therefore, gave up on harmonization, turning instead to the mutual recognition of licenses from other member states. In other words Europe reached and passed a critical watershed. Rather than continuing to meet, unsuccessfully, to reach complex agreements among governments, they changed the agenda to one of requiring governments to create an open and competitive market in all member states. Canadian governments are unwilling to pursue this approach.

One warning is due on international comparisons. Canadians have often looked south for guidance. But in the financial field the results may be unsatisfactory, as the U.S. financial field is not composed of the same types of institutions, the numbers of banks are out of proportion to all other nations, and the regulatory structure is disproportionately thick with regulators, laws, manuals, policies and procedures. The U.S. system is more a branch of law and a study in politics than a well-designed method of regulation. For example, there are over 200 thousand pages of bank laws, regulations and procedures to be complied with. Of these, four thousand change each year on average. The favourable effect on safety and soundness, efficiency and the public interest from the volume of these laws has yet to be demonstrated.

What the U.S. system does show is the politicization of financial regulation. One of the tools which will be used to analyze the Canadian situation is called the public choice approach. This is an economic method which looks at political, bureaucratic or institutional decisions as being based on the incentive systems and motivations of the players. In normal economics these incentives are such things as profits, prices, costs, wages and interest rates. In a public choice analysis the incentives are votes, interest groups, marginal seats and similar factors which exert a powerful influence on non-market determined decision making. The regulation of financial institutions is a subject which interests very few people. Even the academic community has exhibited little consistent interest in financial regulation. Historically economists have been inclined to examine the macroeconomic significance of bank reserve requirements on the money supply rather than the efficiency implications. *Bank Act* revisions can usually elicit a number of learned articles for the occasion. And of those who are inclined to look into such matters, almost none are disinterested. The topic is in the domain of lawyers, accountants, government regulators, self-regulatory bodies such as stock exchanges, politicians, the institutions themselves and the bodies that insure them. Because financial firms are heavily regulated, regulatory changes are sometimes of considerable significance for the range of products which may be sold as well as for the impact on the profitability of competing institutions.

However, the public at large is made better off by good regulation and clearly pays for poor regulation. These costs can be seen in the distribution costs of financial products, the costs arising from protecting market segments from more competition and in the range of choice of financial products available to consumers.

In Canada, the regulation of banks, trust companies, insurance companies, stockbrokers and dealers, as well as other similar bodies, is allocated to the federal government, the ten provinces plus the territories or, indeed, to all of them. If the expression "It's a jungle out there" can truthfully be used to describe without exaggeration a business environment, the regulation of financial institutions would probably qualify.

The reason that the regulatory system is so complex rests on two important facts. First, financial institutions direct the flow of savings and allocate the outstanding stock of financial investments ideally to those uses which maximize the yield, subject to the risk parameters of the investor. It would be a rare government which did not succumb to the temptation either to play a role in this allocation process or to fall prey to interest groups for whom government decisions will direct financial business into their hands. While the financial industry has long had to manage the inherent conflicts of interest which are inescapably part of the intermediation process, it is less frequently remarked that not only are governments subject to such political conflicts on a larger scale but their record in avoiding temptation are far from high standards. Obviously the situation is worse in Canada, with 13 federal, provincial, and territorial governments, than it is in countries such as the United Kingdom or France, with unitary governments.

The second reason for the complexity has to do with changes in the industry since Confederation. There are more financial *products* available to Canadians in the 1990's than there were financial *institutions* in the 1860s. Moreover, technological change has linked markets on a global basis that could not be linked within even a small province in 1867. The current division of powers and the competition among governments have their roots in a frontier economy with limited communications and fewer alternative sources and uses of funds. Fifteen years ago I wrote that "The constitution, as it exists, is more appropriate to a customs union than to a common market."[3] Yet there has never been a reconsideration of the federal-provincial[4] structure in which these industries are regulated.

While there are restrictions to interprovincial trade, there are also problems in the financial products and capital markets area. These are

---

3   John C. Pattison, "Dividing the Power to Regulate" in Thomas Courchene *et al.*, *Canadian Confederation at the Crossroads*, Vancouver: The Fraser Institute, 1978, p. 110.

4   For the sake of editorial convenience "provincial" will be taken to include the territories.

less straightforward barriers to carrying on business across provincial borders.

A simple example of the inefficiencies caused by the federal-provincial regulatory environment may suffice. Banks are federally regulated but in their branches they can sell provincially regulated mutual funds, technically through employees of a provincially regulated subsidiary company. The employees who sell mutual funds must be registered with the provinces and substantial fees must be paid. While those non-bank salesmen who are regularly registered by the province can sell wherever they wish within that single province, bank salespeople can only sell within that branch or another branch. If the bank officer is asked to visit a customer who cannot come to a branch, but who wishes to purchase a mutual fund (for example, an invalid or someone whose work ties them up, such as those in remote towns and other locations) the customer cannot be served by an employee of a bank even if that federal bank employee is also provincially regulated.

Another anomaly is that banks and trust companies are allowed to sell government debt. However, these securities are usually sold in large blocks that make it uneconomic to sell small amounts. One answer is to bundle government debt, such as treasury bills, into "treasury bill mutual funds." However, while the bank can sell the treasury bills it cannot sell the same securities if they are packaged as a mutual fund unless it sets up a provincial subsidiary and subjects itself, and more importantly its customers, to additional costs, additional regulation and additional paperwork, all of which reduce the original yield on the investment.

If this degree of complexity is not enough, it is further compounded by another small group of actors who play an important role in the functioning of the financial system and in structuring the risks and incentives under which the game is played. These are the government insurance agencies such as the Canada Deposit Insurance Corporation and the Canadian Investor Protection Fund.

Who regulates whom?

Whether the federal government, a province or both regulate a financial industry is complex, and indeed, it is even uncertain in some respects. Table 1 illustrates the general rule. However, in reality other layers of government can get involved in the event of insolvency, fraud or other criminal activities, contractual, advertising or marketing considerations. Moreover for every transaction there are at least two sides—a buyer and a seller—if not more. It is possible to have a federally regulated institution on one side of a transaction and a provincially regulated one on another.

The dividing lines are not clear cut. Court decisions have often reaffirmed the current role of one level of government or another. However some decisions have rationally opened up the prospect for a greater federal role in national financial markets as society, technology and financial markets have changed. Unfortunately the uncertainty

Table 1: Who Regulates Whom?

	Federal Jurisdiction	and/ or	Provincial Jurisdiction
Banking	X		—
Insurance	X		X
Trust Companies	X		X
Securities			
a) general	—		X
b) government debt	X		X
c) commercial paper			
i) banks	X		—
ii) other traders	—		X
Investment Management			
a) banks	X		(?)
b) trust companies	X		X
c) other	—		X

Note: At the time of writing, a dispute is brewing between the provincial governments and the federal government, with the banks and trust companies in the middle, over whether federal financial institutions should be able to carry out portfolio management and investment counselling in-house, notwithstanding the federal legislation, or whether these federal institutions should be forced to put these activities into a provincially regulated subsidiary. This explains the question mark in Table 1.

which Canadians are left with, is whether the provinces would yield jurisdiction to one national regulator in preference to twelve local ones or would instead simply persist in their jurisdiction, creating even more overlap.

The simple facts are that there is costly overlap, that the provinces compete with the federal jurisdiction, and that the consumer pays for the regulatory system in the final analysis. These points will be seen throughout this chapter.

Goals of financial regulation

What goals do governments think they can accomplish with financial regulation? Are these regulations cost-effective? Who benefits and who bears the costs? Some of these goals are genuine; some are genuine in principle but are in practice an excuse or justification for the position of a government or an interest group which has found political favour with a government; some are genuine but the laws don't in fact accomplish them; some are in conflict; and they all vary in materiality and relevance in comparison with one another. These goals are, in summary: safety and soundness, competitiveness, efficiency of operation, consumer protection, investor protection, macroeconomic monetary management, exchange rate and interest rate management, allocation of resources within an economy, industrial, regional and small business development, the promotion of government debt finance and equitable access to credit. Not all of these goals are sought simultaneously, depending upon public interest, political imperatives and what problems have arisen. For example, the federal government has used the regulation of interest rates in the past but not in recent years. Similarly, Canada has historically been mercifully free of direct exchange controls compared to other countries.

This section discusses the principles of good regulation. The reader must be alert to the prior question of whether regulation is really called for in the first place. Before one can discuss an appropriate structure for the regulation of any industry it is necessary to have a framework to examine, first, whether there is any justification for any regulation of private activity, any cost-effective argument for intervention in the marketplace, and second, what arguments support a national as opposed to a regional basis for intervention. It is difficult to think of rational arguments for doubly regulating, that is at both the federal and provincial levels.

The goals of the federal and provincial governments are often similar. For example, all levels are concerned with safety and soundness for the financial institutions in their charge. However, the federal government is responsible for the payments system, which is a vital part of Canada's financial infrastructure and of its connection to the international financial markets. This system clears the settlement of payments among the large institutions. Traditionally this has meant the banks and the larger trust companies. However, in recent years concern has grown that the payments system could be put at risk by the failure of a large securities dealer to settle large payments. Such a failure could, in turn, cause the failure of other institutions. This is an international concern. In recent years, U.S. bank supervisors watched carefully over the failure of a large securities dealer for fear of the damage spreading. In Canada the fact that securities companies are provincially regulated, trust companies and insurance companies can be regulated by either or both federal and provincial governments, and the banking and payments systems are federal, does not help manage the risks to the economy stemming from the interdependencies of such key financial groups.

These targets of government policy are interdependent. Sometimes they reinforce one another, at other times they conflict. For example, having a competitive and efficient set of financial firms in an industry may well compete with the prudential goal of safety and soundness. One of the more interesting conflicts has dramatic federal-provincial ramifications. This is the trade-off between investor protection—a provincial responsibility—and safety and soundness, which could be either federal or provincial according to the industry.

One of the instruments used by provincial governments to target investor protection is the concept of "full, plain and true" disclosure of all of the facts which are likely to be a consideration of an investor in making a decision to buy, sell or hold a security. If a publicly traded stockbroker, bank, insurance or trust company was subject to a difficult period in its finances, the institution might well survive or fail not according to its underlying capital but according to whether or not public disclosure had caused a failure of confidence, leading to a liquidity crisis and massive loss of business. Even if one level of government was responsible for both targets these conflicts would remain.

How should the financial regulatory work of the federal government, the provinces and territories be appraised? This is a complex question. Basically it is not a question of determining who is good at their jobs and who is less competent. The skill sets are generally high, although most financial industries complain that there is a lack of industry experience. However, this is not necessarily a valid complaint. Often regulators and the regulatees will be judged unfairly by hindsight as if the outcome of complex financial and economic interdependencies were known in advance.

One of the key questions which should be asked in a complex constitutional setting is whether the locus of regulation is at the appropriate level of government. In my 1978 essay there was a section entitled "Which Level of Government Should Have the Power?" For the present purpose those considerations are valid, but can be refocused in order to examine the regulation of the financial sector in particular. Here the considerations are the efficiency with which policy goals can be achieved by each level of government, mainly because of economies of scale, information costs, and externalities in regulation.

Economies of scale exist when two institutions can be regulated equally well for less than twice the cost of regulating one institution. In addition, regulatory costs can be looked at from the point of view of the regulatee. If the governments have many financial industries to regulate and multiple institutions to implement this strategy, is the overall regulatory cost less if numbers of the governmental regulators are rationalized at both the federal and provincial levels? Logic would suggest that the answer is yes.

In Canada, with our extensive federal and provincial regulatory networks, economies of scale strongly suggest the need for greater rationalization and centralization. Examples abound. In securities regulation, each province duplicates the structure which regulates the underwriting, issuing and trading of securities. Some provinces sensibly do less than others, relying on the external benefits which they pick up from the expenses and activities of some of the other provinces. Nonetheless the cost to each province is excessive, but it is passed on to the suppliers, who have no choice in the matter if they want to do business in the province. A small example of the lack of economies of scale is the reporting of insider trading and the publishing of the resulting trades. An officer of a public company such as a bank files once with the federal government and with seven of the provinces.

An example of the second type of economies of scale concerns the regulation of mutual fund sales by branches of banks and trust companies. The federal *Bank Act* has provisions which require customer disclosure and a means for customers to make complaints if they are not satisfied. The provinces, in order to protect customers once again, require bank mutual fund sales staff to be provincially regulated, registered, examined and subject to police checks. This even applies to the sales of mutual funds composed of bank eligible securities—such as government debt—and where bank sales staff, unlike other securities registrants, can only sell on branch premises. Do the same employees need to have two levels of government regulate their sales practices?

Information costs are a special case of economies of scale. The issue is whether local, that is, provincial, regulators are needed to best serve the interests of local issuers, underwriters, dealers and purchasers and sellers of securities. The argument is often advanced that one national regulator would lose touch with special regional needs. There is justice in the point, especially in a large country such as Canada. However, the point that is never examined is whether this requires separate structures for each province. Since great strides have been made in reducing the variations in the securities laws and regulations, what is needed is simply regional administration, not regional differences in the laws.

Externalities in regulation arise from the overlaps and underlaps. Overlaps exist where more than one government or other type of regulatory institution regulates one activity, thereby imposing additional costs on at least one sector of the industry. For example the issuance of securities prospectuses by federally regulated banks and trust companies is covered by the federal *Bank Act*, the federal *Trust and Loan Companies Act*, and by provincial securities acts. Underlaps occur where no one competently regulates an area or activity, and where there *is* a need to do so. Underlap can occur where an institution from one jurisdiction, its home, has more of its business in another jurisdiction, the host. The danger is that the host may mistakenly assume that the home regulator has full knowledge and awareness. Underlaps may impose costs on other financial firms or on the public in general through the failure of an unregulated or under-regulated firm.

Another consideration in assessing financial regulation is transparency, the ability to see all key decisions by regulators and the reasons for them. Here the provincial securities regulators clearly excel. Investor protection is the primary goal of securities regulation, whereas solvency is the goal of banking, trust and insurance regulation. The latter is often aided by secretiveness rather than transparency. In most cases the hearings and decisions of securities regulators are published almost immediately and full details are often available as to why and how the decision was reached. This is very different from the regulatory decisions by bank, trust and insurance regulators, who may well grant authority in confidence to an individual institution. The differences relate to the different subject matter in front of the different regulators, and to the quasi-judicial nature of decisions by securities commissions.

One of the general distinctions among different forms of regulation is that between functional versus institutional regulation. Functional regulation regulates an activity or a type of transaction. An example is securities regulation. Institutional regulation regulates all activities in that corporate entity. An imperfect example is bank or trust regulation. The Office of the Superintendent of Financial Institutions regulates banks, trust companies and insurance companies. If banks trade in government debt, underwrite commercial paper, or engage in portfolio management and investment counselling, these activities, even though securities related, are governed by federal legislation.

Methods of regulation

In the 1990s the issues at stake in the public debate on the federal and provincial regulation of financial institutions are not those of macroeconomic management. They are mainly those of prudential management: (1) the safety and soundness of the institutions, (2) the powers which they have to carry out their business and (3) how they will be regulated and supervised. These are the order in which the public would probably rank these issues.

However, in order to understand the interplay of these issues it is necessary to start with the third issue.

Regulation versus supervision

Regulation and supervision are related but different concepts. Regulation consists of the applicable laws and regulations passed by Parliaments, Orders-in-Council and other such mechanisms by federal and provincial legislatures. They are legally binding and can have significant legal, financial and penal sanctions and further implications for the ongoing existence of an institution that is caught violating them. The key word is caught. All of the laws that can be committed to paper will not prevent a failure if the financial institution is managed fraudulently or if management of the institution covers up financial problems which should be seen by the internal auditors of the firm, the external shareholders' auditors or the regulators.

Supervision, on the other hand, is the activity of the regulator, often but not always a government, in looking into the operations of a financial institution, analyzing its operations and financial results, interviewing management, inspecting the books, meeting with the internal auditors and other similar tasks in order to assess, and grade, the quality of the institution and the likelihood that it will be able to fulfil its obligations concerning the financial transactions of its customers.

Governments have choices both as to the resources which they commit to overseeing the health of the financial sector in general and to the trade-off in their supply of these resources between regulation and supervision. Given that the costs and benefits are highly skewed between the two, the actual outcome is surprising: both are used extensively. Regulation is inexpensive. Any number of laws can easily and quickly be put on the books. Supervision, on the other hand, requires a significant number of highly trained specialists: lawyers, accountants, auditors, credit analysts, valuation specialists and so forth. These are in scarce supply and tend to be expensive.

Also in favour of regulation over supervision is the fact that politicians and senior government officials better protect their reputation and livelihood by the definitiveness of laws rather than by the probabilistic nature of whether supervision finds the rotten apple in time. In fact there is a further complication. Governments have a political function, a policy making department and a supervisory function. Regulations help the first two but seriously threaten the third. The more laws that are put on the books in the self-interest of the political and policy levels, the greater the onus on the supervisor to monitor carefully compliance with these laws in order to protect his or her own position. These trade-offs are particularly evident in the United States, where not only have enormous volumes of laws been written to protect law makers but there has been evidence of attempts to influence supervisors when the laws threatened local, politically important financial institutions.

In assessing the roles played by different levels of government these trade-offs must be kept constantly in mind. They will be relevant to any reshuffling of powers between federal and provincial governments.

Safety and soundness

The conundrum for both levels of government in providing for the safety and soundness of financial institutions is that if they are not allowed to fail, they will have incentives to follow imprudent practices. If they do fail, they will likely destroy savings, pension and other retirement funds, cash resources of companies, etc., and, in so doing, will cause hardship or poverty, unemployment and possibly the failure of other businesses. This is clearly a trade-off with nothing good to be said about it. The tasks of politicians, governments and financial regulators are not enviable, particularly when they will inevitably be judged in the bright light of hindsight.

It is not possible to describe the complete range of regulatory steps that can be taken in the interests of safety and soundness. In summary these can include minimum start-up capitalization, ongoing capital and liquidity ratios and controls, restrictions on the power of the institutions to carry out transactions of certain types, and restrictions on transactions with affiliated persons and companies which might fall prey to conflicts of interest. Supervision has an equally important role to play in the successful maintenance of safety and soundness.

Powers and organization

Regulation has a lot to do with establishing barriers to reduce competition for the competitive advantage of certain groups. With more regulators there is more scope to shape the laws of economics to protect interest groups at the expense of the general public.

The distinctions in Canada become a matter of competitive advantages and threats, for both the institutions and the regulators. It is vitally important to promote competition, not to hinder it. This means not only allowing all institutions to compete with one another but also requires both entry and exit to the industry. There are many boutiques and other small financial firms that are vital to keeping competition and innovation alive. The challenge for the regulator is that these may also be the most vulnerable. Historically the powers of financial institutions were limited to carrying out only the restricted transactions appropriate to whichever of the four pillars—trust, banking, insurance and securities—was in question. This compartmentalized regulation and made it simpler, and it made the financial industries less competitive. Time and financial innovation (i.e. competition) served to topple the pillars. Stockbrokers, for example, paid interest on cash balances, just like a bank did. Similarly, single premium annuities from insurance companies looked very similar to term deposits. The regulation of trust companies benefitted by the concept of a deposit in trust, which enabled the institution to be provincially regulated even though the savings vehicle is functionally equivalent to a bank deposit.

The new federal financial legislation as applied to federally incorporated banks, trust and insurance companies made a partial step in 1992 to bringing some order out of the collapsing pillars. While not dismantling anywhere near all of the barriers among businesses, it shared more of the powers among these three pillars, whereas securities dealing is the only pillar that is substantially within the provincial domain. However, almost all of the new powers must be carried on in a subsidiary company that can be regulated separately by the provinces or the federal government. This device has enabled federal financial reform to accommodate provincial regulatory interests.

There is some rationale for the use of subsidiaries. Such a structure allocates regulatory and supervisory authority to specialist rather than generalist bodies. It may reduce conflicts of interest if the activities are truly kept separate. However, the price may be unreasonably high even if there is perceived to be a benefit to the regulators. The Law Commission in the United Kingdom has recently written (1992, page 10) that

> There appears to be general agreement that a policy of enforced separation obliging firms to carry on within a separate legal entity only those activities that do not result in conflict is not feasible and in many respects is not desirable. The separate entities would often not be economically viable, certain economies of scale would be lost, the international competitiveness of

United Kingdom financial conglomerates could be impaired and customers could be deprived of the benefits they often obtain from the fact that conglomerates carry on a range of activities.

The Law Commission went on to discuss other legal and regulatory problems with this structure.

Subsidiaries may protect the capital of one type of financial intermediary in the event of a failure by a related institution. However, with this structure there are costs and inefficiencies which reduce the supply of financial products, do not constructively use the extensive national branch and electronic delivery mechanisms of most institutions, not just banks, and which restrict how a customer can be served. For example, clients of different subsidiaries must fill in duplicate forms, supply new information and consent to the exchange of information.

In fact, in the case of insurance, a bank client's right even to contract in law to share information with an insurance subsidiary has been eliminated by regulation. This restriction is not even of general interest to all insurance companies. The main beneficiaries are the very large number of insurance brokers. As a high margin delivery channel, they felt threatened by the lower cost distribution facilities of major bank and trust companies. Hence, they exercised the political prerogatives of a well organized cohesive group with the support of parliament, against the politically unfocused economic interests of the majority of consumers.

While this example may appear self-serving coming from a banker, which it is, its provenance does not detract from its validity. However, there is another side to this issue which is worth noting. One of the good things which can come out of an excess of regulatory jurisdictions can be competition. Some governments may feel that the public interest is better served by more competition. There have been benefits in Canada where a province took a more liberal attitude. Quebec has often done so in the financial regulatory field. If Quebec had not allowed a federally regulated bank to acquire a provincially incorporated securities company, it is probably fair to say that deregulation would have occurred several years later than it did. As it happened, the action of Quebec forced the hands of both Ontario and the federal government. This argument cannot be taken too far for the reasons of efficiency mentioned earlier. Too many jurisdictions would raise costs and the level of regulation without any compensating benefit.

The subsidiary structure is designed to support regulation by function as opposed to institutional regulation. In Canada, functional means mainly, but not entirely, provincial regulation. However, notwithstanding the changes in the powers of financial institutions, regulatory systems are still designed around the core functions of each industry. This gives rise to monumental challenges of co-operation and information sharing, the bulk of which is made more difficult either by crossing provincial geographical lines or the federal-provincial regulatory divide.

In concluding this section on methods of regulation, there is another distinction which needs to be made. Regulation and supervision can be carried out either by a government or by what is called a self regulatory organization, or "SRO." The theory is that in some markets the degree of industry knowledge and transactional scrutiny is so great that only the industry can, within certain parameters, set up an independent organization to regulate itself. SRO's are almost exclusively provincial, rather than federal, and include the stock exchanges and the Investment Dealers Association. In the following section on the regulation of securities activities this distinction will be explored in more detail.

The regulation of securities activities

The regulation of securities transactions is one of the more fascinating areas of financial regulation. It is carried out extensively by lawyers, yet it involves detailed scrutiny of individual financial transactions and players. It is challenged by the transactions of the industry, yet often defers to the self-regulatory bodies of the industry itself. It is provincially regulated yet, although there are exceptions, in many areas it has "cookie-cutter" regularity across jurisdictions. It does not want to be dominated by Ontario, which has the largest share of securities and capital markets activity, yet other provinces will, sensibly, often wait for Ontario to write its regulations. Multiplication of many functions, such as insider-reporting, is standard as provinces have reflected a lack of total trust in the rigour of some of their compatriots in enforcing the insider trading reporting requirements. The details of the history of the development of the current provincial system are well described in Anisman (1986).

What a security actually is, on the one hand is almost a metaphysical concept, yet pragmatically it is whatever a provincial securities commission says it is. A senior federal Department of Finance official once suggested to the author that "a security is anything that isn't a cow." On the other hand, a bank can originate a loan and sell the loan to other legal entities. Further, in international markets, in order to sell and transfer ownership in some large marketable international loans, these syndicated loans come with transferable loan certificates. However these are not securities in law and have always been recognized as credit transactions. Yet in Canada securities and banking law have seriously restricted or prohibited a bank doing a private placement for the debt of a customer which is, in many ways, very similar to the above types of transactions. It should be noted that even the highly regimented U.S. banking system allows a bank to do private placements as an agent. These uncertainties and conflicts restrict the number and types of transactions for fear of triggering the regulation of a deal by securities regulators, particularly if the transaction could transgress the artificial dividing line that separates the powers of a provincial securities company from, for example, those of a federally regulated bank.

However, it is of vital importance to know when a transaction either involves a security or may be regulated by a provincial securities commission. Consider the example of foreign exchange. Foreign exchange transactions are not securities transactions. However, an option on the future exchange rate traded on an exchange can be regulated as a security. Some markets are in the domain of both the federal and provincial governments. An example is the underwriting, trading and distributing of government debt. A federally regulated bank can carry out this activity, or it can be done by a provincial securities company. Because there is little or no risk to the principal of an investor in government debt, and because of the need to mobilize the nationwide resources of banks to finance governments, this overlap is not controversial.

Securities regulation has goals which are meritorious but which have been criticized as being, on occasion, too all-encompassing. For example, securities regulation registers salespeople and dictates how the securities can be sold. It also provides for the approval of each product itself in the form of prospectuses for new issues of securities. Educational requirements and other proficiency standards are precisely determined for those who are registered to sell and/or advise. There are rules for companies which issue securities and rules concerning disclosure of information.

The provinces prohibit or severely limit the ability of residents of a province to deal with an institution or salesman in another province or country. A consumer who wants to deal with an institution from outside the province cannot even voluntarily decline the protection of the province. As a result a monumental interprovincial barrier to trade is created. In addition provincial securities law purports to regulate foreign institutions dealing with provincial residents even when they are outside Canada as for instance with portfolio management services.

Several years ago Ontario put in place a regime of "Universal Registration" requiring virtually anyone who dealt in securities, other than an investor, to be regulated in one form or another. This would have eliminated the so-called exempt market in which certain types of institutions could deal in certain types of transactions without registration. Ontario has been the most zealous advocate of this approach, with other provinces being more open. This stance is felt to be strongly protectionist, under the disguise of the ostensible policy goal of investor protection.

One question for governments, securities regulators and those who trade in securities is whether such an all-embracing approach to regulation is necessary. This is a question of more general interest than this article but it is a question which must be asked. The costs of such an extensive regulatory system are the cash costs of running the regulatory apparatus plus the cost of satisfying all of the legal, operational, disclosure and other costs of the users of the system plus the welfare costs of transactions which do not occur because of the extent of regulation in excess of that required for investor protection.

One of the considerations is that investors must be prudent in reaching their own investment decisions. No amount of regulation will stop investors losing money or receiving bad advice. While the current extent of regulation cannot prevent this result either, it does produce a costly and heavily burdened sector.

Not all provinces feel the same way about the extent of required securities regulation. While Ontario has been moving to universal registration, British Columbia has been taking a more liberal approach in order to encourage risk-taking, particularly in the resource sector which is important to the province.

An assessment

The question for the purposes of this book is what is the impact of provincial regulation of securities activities? The simple answer is that, on the positive side, the current system is properly administered with standards and supervision by highly qualified and competent staff. However, there are problems with the current setup that are not inconsequential. The largest of these is the uncertainty that such a regime is called for in the first instance or generates benefits which exceed the heavy costs of the high degree of intervention. As noted earlier, these forms of provincial regulation generate enormous barriers to trade and to capital flows as well as limiting the ability to do many kinds of transactions even within a province. Some more detailed observations are also called for.

First, the present system is awkward and expensive because ten provinces and two territories are involved. Although most of the transactions will occur in a few of the provinces, the costs of duplication, registration and the delays, inconvenience and lack of national standards are all experienced by national institutions. There are several mechanisms for interprovincial consultation and harmonization. One vehicle is a group called the Canadian Securities Administrators ("CSA"). The CSA meets formally twice a year and has working groups which attempt to resolve complex issues. Although the quality of the staff who attend these meetings is high, the CSA suffers from some severe drawbacks. The CSA is only composed of regulators. While they do selectively entertain submissions from outside bodies, it is definitely a clearing-house for the regulators, without a balanced recognition of the interests of consumers or any attempt whatsoever to do any cost-benefit calculation on its positions.

By meeting infrequently with no permanent infrastructure or method of determining solutions other than unanimity, the CSA always seems to be facing an uphill task. Moreover, because unanimity rather than voting is the decision rule, harmonization that can be achieved is either of a lower order than desirable or leaves provinces opting out or making their own choices outside of the CSA framework. If one or more provinces can successfully argue for a CSA policy it may well add to the overall burden of regulation across the country without representation by consumers or a test as to justification.

A second problem is that the overlap with the regulation of other financial industry groups, either within a province or in a federal-provincial setting, is unresolved. Not only are there conflicts between regulators, particularly at the federal-provincial level, but the companies which find themselves at the junction of these two regulators are hard put to find a way to lessen the burden of regulation or to seek effective ways for better regulation. To return to an earlier example, federal bank and trust company sales of money market mutual funds are, to consumers, effectively a type of deposit substitute. In a better world the distribution of these products would be regulated by bank regulators as a branch activity. However, in the current environment these products are sold in a way that has high regulatory costs which are borne by the consumer. An important point to ponder is that the consumers of these mutual funds have not sought regulation, nor have there been complaints or scandals leading to such regulation. This is gratuitous regulation at its worst. It happens simply because of the overlap of jurisdictions, as regulators seek to compete using the laws and regulations given to them in a different setting for different purposes.

A third problem is that an increasingly large number of regulatory issues are arising at the international level, not the provincial one. Examples include multi-jurisdictional disclosure (the ability to use national offering documents, such as prospectuses, in the sale of the same securities in the United States or Canada), inter-governmental agreements on information sharing, insider trading, capital requirements and other detailed areas of regulation. Canada has no national securities laws aside from those that impact federal banks, trust and insurance companies.

The technology of the financial marketplace, especially that of electronic trading and communications, illustrates that whatever the historical reasons for most securities powers being regulated by twelve provincial and territorial governments, the justification for such an arrangement today is not readily apparent. The markets are global, not provincial, and the time-frame for transactions is the speed of light, not the telegraph or road link to the provincial border as might have been the case in 1867.

An example of the difficulties experienced by our chaotic system of overlapping regulations was evident in the 1980s in the process of deregulation. The provinces agreed to allow foreign access to Canadian securities markets prior to the North American Free Trade Agreement. Consequently, Canada was left with no bargaining chips, having already given them away at the provincial level. Well prior to the free trade negotiations the authors of the Dupré report had warned[5] that "The measures proposed by the OSC would require an open and formal change in government policy on domestic control that is for the Cabinet to determine and that in our view should be weighed in the context of Canada's impending bilateral and multilateral trade negotiations."

The regulation of trust companies

In order to discuss the regulation of trust companies it is necessary to know what they are and what they are not. The general public probably views trust companies as another type of bank. While such an observation is wrong on its technical merits, it is unlikely that a typical consumer sees much difference between the two types of institutions. However, even a consumer who is indifferent between institutions should be aware of the vital differences between his or her deposit with a bank and a similar transaction with a trust company. These differences relate to the legal basis on which each type of institution accepts a deposit, which in turn determines the applicable type of regulation.

The word trust in the name of a trust company says it all. A trust company accepts deposits only as "guaranteed trust money." These trust deposits take priority over the claims of all other creditors in the event of an insolvency by a trust company. The trust company must also

---

5   Task force members, J. Stefan Dupré, Chairman, A Rendall Dick, Q.C. and Alexander J. MacIntosh, Q.C., *The Ontario Task Force on Financial Institutions—Final Report*, Ontario, December 1985, p. 6.

designate assets to be held against these trust deposits. On the other hand a deposit with a bank is treated simply as a debtor-creditor relationship. The deposits are the property of the bank, which has the obligation to repay them. While these differences may appear technical they also have a significant impact on the operations of a trust company. The differences "straddle a constitutional crack in the regulatory process" as Best and Shortell put it in *A Matter of Trust* (1985, p. 13), because the duty of trusts falls under provincial responsibility while "banking" is a federal jurisdiction.

The other element in the word trust is the concept of a fiduciary, that is the ability to be a trustee. A trustee handles property including money and investments on behalf of another in a special relationship that is carefully defined and interpreted in law and where special duties of care are legally binding. The trustee usually has legal title to the assets. However, the trustee is the steward, looking after the assets for the benefit of the beneficiaries of the trust. This means that a trust company can act as a trustee for a trust, as an executor of an estate, as an administrator of assets held in trust or as an official guardian or in a similar role. These are powers which only trust companies are allowed to carry out in Canada.

Another factor which must be faced in the regulation of trust companies is the historical vulnerability of some of these companies to serious, and sometimes fatal, financial and management problems. This weakness has led to some key issues in their regulation.[6] The federal-provincial overlaps and underlaps are an integral part of this story built from cases of trust companies that survived and prospered and those that failed.

To illustrate the nature of feelings concerning federal-provincial regulatory matters, Best and Shortell (p. 281) tell the story of how Alberta Consumer Minister Connie Osterman thought that she

---

6   A readable source of information in the trust industry to the mid-1980s is provided by Best and Shortell. They provide a wealth of information on many of the companies in the trust business, its various federal and provincial regulators and the role of the insurers such as the Canada Deposit Insurance Corporation.

had valid complaints about federal—and Ontario—regulators' treatment of Alberta incorporated companies. Her trust industry people were protecting home grown companies against Ottawa's aggressive advances . . . Their Ottawa counterparts didn't like having the provinces in the business of regulating financial institutions.

Best and Shortell went on to report (p. 281-82) that "one slightly paranoid provincial official opined in early 1985 that the reason more small trust companies would be allowed to go under was that Ottawa was not displeased when the provinces looked foolish." They also reported (p. 331) "The debate about deregulating financial institutions isn't just about companies fighting for turf; it's also about governments scrapping for territory."

Disputes between governments and the impact that these have on regulation go to the heart of a system where the social and political costs of the failure of an institution may occur in jurisdictions other than that of the home regulator. In the late 1980s the Principal Group of Companies, which was based in Alberta, ran into problems involving its sales practices, its management activities and its solvency. These had been building up over time, and officials in the government of Alberta had become aware of some of the difficulties. However when Alberta was forced to act, the impact was felt not only in Alberta but also in British Columbia and the Maritimes as well. This concentrates the minds of provincial governments when allowing out-of-province trust companies to do business. Concerns for solvency and interprovincial competition can conflict in such circumstances.

At an earlier date, Ontario had taken this concern with failures to heart as a result of criticism over the failure of numerous trust companies. The 1988 *Loan and Trust Corporations Act* required that any trust company operating in Ontario would have to comply with Ontario regulations in all of its operations, not just those in Ontario. This thrust is called the "equals approach." It has an impact on federal and provincial trust and loan companies with extra-territorial effect. While seemingly draconian and hostile to institutions in other provinces, it was based on the rationale that tougher legislation in Ontario alone would drive some institutions to seek a more convenient and lenient province for their home regulator. Other provinces such as Alberta and British Columbia use an alternative referred to as the "designated jurisdiction"

approach, conceding to the home regulator in the province of incorpo-
ration the primary responsibility for the regulation of the out-of-province trust company in their host jurisdiction.

Ontario's actions have fuelled considerable criticism of the
province's actions. Ontario was quite simply saying that it didn't trust
the quality of regulation or the motivation in other provinces. However
in so doing it erected a trade barrier to protect the rich Ontario market
from out-of-province competitors unless they added a new layer of
regulation as the price for doing business in Ontario. On an incremental
basis this is very costly, particularly for smaller companies from other
provinces trying to grow by building a client base in Ontario.

An assessment

Trust companies have had an unreasonably high mortality rate. To some
extent this is because of the small size of many of these institutions,
which has been encouraged by the regional regulatory structure as a
barrier to a national market;it is also because of the costs of regulation
by each province and also by the federal government. The trust industry
has both a small number of large institutions that are on the whole well
run, in good shape and of reasonable economies of scale, and a much
larger number of smaller institutions some of which from time to time
have had their problems. Some of these problems have stemmed from
the volatility of interest rates and hence the difficulties of matching the
terms of assets and liabilities. Smaller institutions also cannot diversify
risk as well as larger institutions, and they may be more dependent upon
a region or an industry. Some institutions, because of controlling shareholders, have been prone to "self-dealing," that is, carrying out transactions with the owners or the owners' companies on a basis that is not at
arm's length pricing.

Yet governments and regulators quite rightly want to support entry
into the industry in order to foster competition and the growth of the
financial industry. It is not an easy task, and it is made worse by the
overlapping regulatory structure.

The overlapping forms of regulation, particularly when the overlap
involves Ontario and its "equals approach" make life very difficult for
the institutions. The overlaps and conflicts between the Ontario Act and
the new federal trust and loans legislation restrict the abilities of federal

trust companies to do certain kinds of transactions, such as letters of credit and certain types of guarantees, while creating a difficult environment in which to assure compliance with the different acts. The interaction of the two restricts such things as the ways in which a federal trust company can fund itself or how the leverage of its capital can be utilized. Investment standards also differ, as do many other details. Nonetheless these are the price for having an Ontario presence in the trust industry.

Only an unemployed constitutional lawyer could learn to love this structure of regulation. As someone who is not a lawyer, I find it strange that with property and civil rights being provincial powers and being the basis for their regulation of trust companies, we can also quite successfully have federal trust companies legislation (presumably because of interprovincial transactions). It is equally strange that institutions that compete with and are very similar to federal banks in their business activities are regulated provincially. Moreover, given the conflicts among the jurisdictions and the impediments to competition, it cannot have been an easy time for those larger trust institutions whose goals are to offer nation-wide service to their customers.

The added dimension of deposit insurance

Deposit insurance is offered by the Canada Deposit Insurance Corporation (CDIC), a federal government crown corporation, and by the Regie de l'Assurance-dépôts du Quebec (RADQ). The member companies of CDIC are federally incorporated banks and trust and loan companies as well as provincially incorporated trust and loan companies. In mid-1992 the membership was composed of 61 banks, 49 federal trust and loan companies and 31 provincial trust and loan companies.[7]

It is not an enviable position to be an insurer for institutions that are regulated by a different level of government and where the other government may have interests very different from that of the insurer. There is the potential for a classic conflict of interest in which one level of government could encourage growth of regionally based trust com-

---

7   See *CDIC Annual Report 1991*, March 31, 1992, page 9.

panies knowing that another level of government would pay for its mistakes. As Daniels notes (page 5) "until only recently, the federal government has picked up the full tab for financial institution failures, even when the institution was provincially chartered." In fact, since any CDIC payouts are funded by a levy on its members, the ultimate longer run costs of the failure are borne by consumers of surviving institutions as a whole.

So one of the effects of our current insurance arrangements is to encourage the establishment of regional institutions, which have a higher probability of failure than national institutions. The establishment of these firms may also accommodate provincial political interests. But the result is to distort the flows of capital in Canada, to encourage higher risk ventures that experience has now shown to have a lower, not a higher, rate of return on the investment. Combined with the inefficiencies of regulation this structure creates distorted financial markets rather than efficient ones. Ultimately the consumer alone pays the CDIC premiums which cover the cost of the failures.

Bill C-48 was recently passed by the House of Commons to effect amendments to the CDIC Act. One of the effects of this bill would be "significant assistance to CDIC in dealing with federal member institutions which the Superintendent of Financial Institutions determines are, or are about to become, no longer viable". While the federal company will bear the initial costs of a provincial failure, its activities to avoid either failures or their costs are not facilitated by the split regulatory authority over trust and loan companies.

Policy alternatives

The easiest alternative in the complex Canadian constitutional and regulatory situation is to do nothing and to ignore the problems. While the regulatory structure is not elegant, or even pretty, it does function at an administrative level. As mentioned earlier, the quality of the supervision is high in many provinces and at the federal level, although not universally. The losers are consumers and many institutions whose votes and political influence are scattered.

However, there is no justification for much of this regulation. It is not demanded by consumers or sought by parliament in a well thought out manner that reflects the national interests rather than the interests of the thirteen competing regulators. There has been no attempt to justify the form, substance, extent or structure of the increasingly unwieldy machinery of regulation. Recently some provinces have shown an interest in revisiting the regulatory agenda but not much can be expected from a regionally piecemeal approach to a national issue.

It is not surprising that the growth of regulation has a life of its own irrespective of the public interest. The argument to do something must be based on the facts that the current system is costly, reduces consumer choices and hinders the ability of institutions to service clients across provincial boundaries. Another reason for change is that the provincial and federal governments are all working with excessive and even crippling deficits which severely limit their ability to spend more money on regulating these industries. Yet if the provinces were divisions of a company much of the overlap would be eliminated, although regional sales offices would continue to service local clients.

Activities are currently taking place to make the current system function better. However, rather than reducing regulation, the goals are often to make the process better for regulators. The costs or the benefits or justifications for regulation are the places to begin, but they are almost never considered by governments or regulators. The benefits of the marketplace are often totally neglected. One reason for this dismal situation is the nature of the political process. Any single instance of a problem in financial markets will be seen as a failure by the politicians, the regulators or both. As a consequence, self protection leads to excessive regulation out of line with the probability of occurrence or any cost-benefit calculations. And then the approach to excess is to harmonize it.

Under the general guise of harmonization, trust, securities, insurance, bank and other regulators meet regularly as noted earlier. The Toronto Stock Exchange and the Investment Dealers Association ("IDA") are working on a plan to place primary regulatory jurisdiction with the IDA rather than continue the current system where this function is carried out by the four stock exchanges and the IDA. The current system results in a duplication of costs. The IDA has a conflict of interest as it is an industry association, a lobbyist, in addition to being an SRO. Plans are afoot to move the lobbyist function to another body. The other three stock exchanges are apparently reluctant to give up their regulatory functions over their members, so the final outcome is unknown at the time of writing. Another recent initiative has been an agreement to create a Maritime Securities Commission which will, if the plan succeeds, administer a uniform securities act and regulations for the four maritime provinces.

There have been no attempts to reduce unnecessary regulation even though every financial institution and industry body has a shopping list of such changes. One reason is the fear that nothing can be done, both because of the overlap between the federal and provincial governments and because of the difficulty of inducing twelve provinces and territories to change. The Ontario "Equals Approach" should be an early casualty. The securities regulators must eliminate the interprovincial and international barriers. Overlapping layers should be eliminated surgically—there is no magic to cutting an overlap. However, the detailed legalistic nature of regulation will unfortunately give rise to meticulous and costly line-by-line negotiation of changes. What this points out, however, is the need to change the way of dealing with the problem itself, a conclusion the members of the European Community reached long ago.

There are some other alternatives which could also be examined.

National Securities Commission—National Banking Regulator

Since Canada is one of the few countries without a national securities regulator of some kind, and since other countries have recently created them (Australia), or improved them (France), why doesn't Canada move in that direction? Similarly, if a federal deposit insurer will take the hit for failures of institutions in nine provinces why don't we also consolidate the supervision and regulation of banks and trust companies? However we should also ask if we want all of this regulation in the first place.

No one wants overlapping regulation except the regulator who may be displaced. The consumers do not want it, and the companies in the industry do not want it. However, many groups in addition to the regulators themselves profit from a complex system with many jurisdictions. The legal profession, as a whole, benefits by making up to 12 filings where one might do. There is also more work for accountants.

Recently two lawyers, Timothy Unwin and Greg Warren, have written a useful and informative assessment of whether there may be a new phase in this issue of establishing a national securities agency. They examine events since the Hockin-Kwinter Accord of 1987. This was an agreement between Ottawa and Ontario to agree on their responsibilities for regulating securities activities of federal financial institutions. Unwin and Warren make three important points on the constitutional side. First, they note that "there is little doubt that there is a valid constitutional basis for comprehensive federal securities legislation" (page 26). They base this on legal experts' views and legal cases which support federal trade and commerce power and jurisdiction over interprovincial trade.

Second, they note the limitations which will impair provincial regulatory abilities as securities markets expand nationally and internationally. Third, because of the current situation of concurrent jurisdictions, they note that the "effective development of a national scheme for securities regulation will be best achieved through federal-provincial co-operation" (p. 27).

It is hard not to believe that time will eventually lead to a proper national system for Canada, if only to eliminate barriers to interprovincial securities dealings. Small steps in that direction are already evident in the plans of the IDA referred to above, the decision of the Maritime provincial governments, and the growing role of federally regulated banks active from coast to coast. However, we must keep in mind that overlapping regulation would be the worst outcome from an incompetently organized push for federal securities regulation.

The radical view would be to have minimal or no regulation. However, even if this proposition was supported by a cost-benefit calculation, which it might well be, politicians would be threatened by this situation as the opposition would aggressively criticize a government for any difficulty which occurred.

From harmonization to mutual recognition

The European Community has introduced plans and legislation to create a European market for financial services. In the deposit-taking area these plans in the Second Banking Directive deal with the similarities of institutions and the difficulties of trying to define markets by using the names of types of institutions. As a consequence the legislation will apply to "credit institutions," which would catch banks, trust companies and credit unions if applied in Canada.[8]

The Second Directive permits licensed institutions to establish branches (not subsidiaries) in any other member country and to do business in any country. This mutual recognition of licenses is applicable for a list of activities impressive in its breadth. It includes all the traditional banking services plus such activities as underwriting, dealing in securities, portfolio management and advice, financial futures and options and leasing. But this regulatory structure is more complex than it appears at first glance; the ramifications are well explored in Gruson and Nikowitz and the business ramifications are examined in Pattison (1990).

The move to mutual recognition and a single license were occasioned by a situation very much like the Canadian one. The existence of legislation and regulation in twelve countries reduced competition and consumer choice while complicating the purchase and sale of financial products by all concerned. Europe, unlike Canada, at least aimed at creating a single market. This structure, like Canada's, resisted reasonable attempts at reasonable harmonization, leading to the powerful device of mutual recognition.

In Canada mutual recognition would fall afoul immediately of Ontario and the equals approach but would be acceptable to a number of provincial governments. Pierre Fortier, previously a cabinet minister in the government of Quebec, had spoken favourably on the European

---

8   Much of this concerns the Second Banking Directive referred to in the article by Gruson and Nikowitz. There are other directives dealing with other segments of the financial industry. However, in the interests of economy only credit institutions will be discussed here.

structure while in charge of financial institutions in Quebec.[9] However, given Canada's historic inability to agree to solutions which cross provincial boundaries, this mechanism is unlikely to find political success in Canada even though it currently works for 12 European countries of far greater complexity and diversity than Canada. As Professor Daniels points out (page 10) in discussing the problems of mutual recognition "The fact that the Equals Approach remains in force, despite a number of changes in the content of the financial institutions regulations of many of the participating governments, underscores the difficulties in building a horse by committee."

The Australian Securities Commission: a case study

Australia had had many of the same problems as Canada with federal-state conflicts. Prior to the establishment of the Australian Securities Commission, its predecessor the National Companies and Securities Commission had serious flaws relative to the execution of its mandate. As in Canada, political control and accountability were fragmented with no government or minister responsible for the successful functioning of the financial sector. And the Australian States had wanted to keep political and administrative control over this national and international activity, but the tensions in this scheme led to its inevitable and logical downfall.

In 1987 the Australian Senate examined the previous system and pronounced it deficient. As a result the federal, Commonwealth, government, by one federal *Corporations Act 1989*, set up a system to replace the previous "co-operative" companies law and securities regulatory scheme with a single national regulatory authority, the Australian Securities Commission, covering all of the States and the Northern Territory. Any future amendments to the *Corporations Act* will automatically apply in all States and the Northern Territory. All securities

---

9   See Pierre Fortier, "Towards Harmonization of Canadian Policies," Address to the Financial Services Institute, Toronto, November 29, 1988. He notes (page 11) "In Canada, we would do well to follow the example of the EEC."

licenses issued by a state will now be valid throughout Australia. This would bring a big improvement to competition if adopted in Canada.

The implementation of these arrangements is extremely complex from a constitutional law point of view *and* is operationally complex in effecting the changes in the courts and in the administration of the securities laws, especially given the pre-existing structure and cases for investigation or prosecution which pre-dated the changes. What is encouraging is that the Australian example shows that complex change is possible in a federal-provincial structure.

Conclusion and recommendation

I offer one set of conclusions on the facts, one on the future and a recommendation. On the facts, Canada has barriers to financial transactions across provincial boundaries. The costs and inefficiencies of financial regulation in Canada to consumers, investors, borrowers and others is out of proportion to any benefits, yet no one bothers to justify new regulations let alone old ones on a cost benefit basis. Also, global markets and the danger of the transmission of financial risk through the payments system indicate strongly that the existing Canadian financial regulatory system is outdated. Another fact is that the much-heralded process of harmonization is an apology for the current situation, not its solution. It not only supports unjustified regulations, but generally leads to harmonization on the lowest common denominator, or to provinces opting out to introduce their own rules. Also, the current system represents both good and bad forms of regulatory competition. Governments compete to maintain their regulatory reach and often the fees from regulation. Sometimes industries exploit this competition to seek a less well regulated home. For safety and soundness reasons this has pushed governments into positions, such as Ontario's Equals Approach, where they attempt to apply local law extraterritorially in order to protect their province from the failure of an out-of-province institution. As reported earlier, the current system is neither elegant nor pretty.

Regulators need to be examined for their impact on the marketplace and regulations for their benefit-cost contribution. The biggest cost is a loss of competition through barriers to trade, the layering of costs and the distortion of incentives.

On the future the likelihood is that past processes will generate little incremental progress relative to the incremental efforts required. The widely held view is that since the provinces and the federal government are well entrenched in what they perceive to be desirable, risk averse constitutional niches, progress will come from cooperation. However, there are rapidly diminishing returns to cooperation, that is, most of the regulatory gains can be achieved early on.[10]

The recommendation is that a bold initiative is needed to make the quantum leap to unite need with reality. It has been said that politicians will do the right thing after exhausting all the alternatives. If the Australian example is considered there is only one reason why such an approach would not work here: that is, that provincial governments do indeed want to regulate local financial markets as if they had independent national financial systems and the protection of their local industry as their political goals.

The bold stroke in Canada would be to lower the overall burden of financial regulation. It is achievable. Not only would this expand internal Canadian markets but it would help the Canadian financial industry compete against the U.S. industry, which is a growing threat. That would be constructive competition for the regulatory system.

---

10   The gains from cooperation can be analyzed. It is a market like any other. For a parallel analysis using the theory of clubs see Fratianni and Pattison (1982).

Bibliography

Anisman, Philip, "The Regulation of the Securities Market and the Harmonization of Provincial Laws" in Cumming, 1986, 77-168.

Best, Patricia and Ann Shortell, *A Matter of Trust*, Penguin Books, Markham, 1985.

Coleman, William D., "Financial Services Reform in Canada: The Evolution of Policy Dissension," *Canadian Public Policy—Analyse de Politiques*, XVIII, 2, 1992, 139-152.

Cumming, Ronald C., *Harmonization of Business Law in Canada*, University of Toronto Press, Toronto, 1986.

Canada Deposit Insurance Corporation, *Annual Report 1991*, a report by the Chairman Don McKinlay to the Honourable John McDermid, Minister of State (Finance and Privatization), March 31, 1992.

Daniels, Ronald J., "Breaking the Log-Jam: How to Move Beyond the Equals Approach," remarks presented at the Institute for International Research Conference on the New Financial Services Regulations, February 25-26, 1992.

Gruson, Michael and Werner Nikowitz, "The Second Banking Directive of the European Economic Community and Its Importance for Non-EEC Banks," *Fordham International Law Journal*, Vol. 12, No. 2, Winter 1989, 205-241.

Fratianni, Michele and John Pattison, "The Economics of International Organizations," *Kyklos*, 35, 2, 1982, 244-262.

The Law Commission, *Fiduciary Duties and Regulatory Rules: A Summary*, Consultation Paper No. 124 (summary), HMSO, London, England, 1992.

Pattison, John C., "Dividing the Power to Regulate," in Thomas Courchene *et al.*, *Canadian Confederation at the Crossroads*, The Fraser Institute, Vancouver, 1978.

Pattison, John C., "Bank Marketing Strategies in the EC," Chapter 8 in John A. Quelch, Robert D. Buzzell and Eric Salama, *The Marketing Challenge of Europe 1992*, Addison-Wesley Publishing Company, Reading, Massachusetts, 1990.

Pattison, John C., "The Management of Regulatory Risk in Banking: An International Perspective," *The G-7 Report*, May 1992, 45-58.

Unwin, Timothy N. and Greg Warren, "Towards a Federal Securities Law?" *Canadian Financial Services Alert*, Volume 5, Number 4, August 1992, 25-28.

Interprovincial Barriers to Agricultural Trade

**Barry E. Prentice,
Professional Associate,
Transport Institute and
Associate Professor, Dept.
of Agricultural Economics,
University of Manitoba**[1]

W HEN TRADE-DISTORTING MEASURES ARE USED to improve the relative incomes of farmers, almost everyone else seems to end up worse off. Moreover, the total losses to society are generally far greater than the gains of the privileged few. This phenomenon has been amply

1   The author is grateful to Dr. Arthur G. Wilson, Dr. Elmer L. Menzie, Dr. R.M.A. Loyns and an anonymous reviewer for their constructive comments on a previous draft. The content of the paper is the sole responsibility of the author.

demonstrated in international trade, and in the case of Canada, by the barriers to interprovincial trade in agricultural products.

Since the mid-1980s, the issue of "free trade within Canada" has been gaining political momentum. Interprovincial trade barriers have been addressed repeatedly at First Ministers' conferences, and in the communiques that have been issued following high level meetings of federal and provincial agricultural ministers. The expanding chorus of pledges to deal with measures that distort interprovincial trade suggest increasing political commitment. The process of actually eliminating these barriers however, suffers a profound inertia.

The problem of interprovincial barriers to agricultural trade continues to attract public attention. The debate is being fuelled by a growing body of literature that documents the plethora of agricultural subsidies, discriminatory practices, and regulations that distort interprovincial trade. The purpose of this essay is to examine the scope of interprovincial barriers to agricultural trade, and the progress that has been made to eliminate, or reduce these distortions. The discussion begins with the presentation of a conceptual framework to analyze trade barriers.

Barriers to trade

Discussions of interprovincial barriers to trade are often frustrated by the lack of precise definitions. Barriers to trade are comprised of "natural" obstacles and "man-made" hindrances. The "natural" obstacles are the actual costs of the resources used to conduct sales in an external market. The "man-made" hindrances are the government programs and regulations that add to the costs of trade, or discriminate against external suppliers relative to local producers. Some "man-made" hindrances, such as customs tariffs that affect international trade, are highly visible, but most interprovincial trade barriers take the form of non-tariff measures in which a "man-made" hindrance is combined with a "natural" obstacle and disguised from view. As a result, it is often difficult to be exact about where interprovincial barriers begin and end. Figure 1 presents a conceptual model that illustrates the "natural" and "man-made" roots of interprovincial trade barriers.

Natural barriers

The "natural" obstacles to trade include the logistical costs associated with selling products in a distant market, such as transportation, packaging, storage, inventory shrinkage, control and trade financing. In addition, there are transaction costs involved with overcoming the frictions of distance. These transaction costs may entail the need to prepare for operations in a different language, foreign currency exchange fees, charges for long distance telecommunication, and the costs of maintaining a field sales staff.

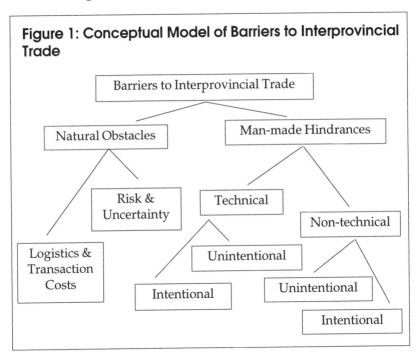

Figure 1: Conceptual Model of Barriers to Interprovincial Trade

In addition to the higher physical costs of conducting external trade, the business risks are often more difficult to judge. The greater uncertainty of success associated with operations in a distant market creates an intangible barrier to trade. The "natural" obstacle presented by uncertainty can only be overcome through efforts to study and invest in information that reduces risk, or through a premium price for the product that compensates for the higher risk. In either case, this intangible barrier has a real effect as an impediment to trade.

Man-made barriers

Proximity to markets always provides local producers with a cost
advantage because the "natural" obstacles are easier to overcome. But
politicians have often yielded to the requests of interest groups to create
additional protection through regulations and licences that add to the
cost, or block the entry of competing goods. These are direct forms of
"man-made" hindrances, but protection of a market can also be
achieved indirectly, by subsidizing local producers.

"Man-made" hindrances can be divided into technical and non-
technical categories. Technical hindrances are special regulations that
require outside suppliers to alter the preparation of their product for
sale in the local market. The alteration may involve different labelling,
grading, packaging or specific preparation (e.g exclusion of some chemical). The impact of a technical impediment is particular to the product
or commodity, and can normally be overcome, at some added cost to
the outside supplier. Although most technical impediments exaggerate
some logistical cost, they can also be directed at increasing the risk or
uncertainty of trade. For example, if a shipper is subject to unpredictable
inspections that delay movements and increase the risk of damage, or
the risk of a lost sale, this can deter entry into a market.

Non-technical impediments are broader in scope and are designed
to discriminate in favour of producers within defined political boundaries. Typically, non-technical impediments operate through an entitle-
ment system that distributes a subsidy, or an indirect income transfer,
to the local producers. Outside parties are not eligible for these payments and can face other restrictions. The artificial separation of markets
distorts the price system. As a result, the impacts of non-technical
impediments can extend beyond the target groups and affect other
parties in the local marketing chain, as well as outside competitors.

In some cases, great ingenuity has been applied to the creation of
measures that distort trade. There are instances however, where the
trade effects are a secondary, or unintentional, aspect of a policy that
was devised to serve a legitimate need. The boundary between "intentional" and "unintentional" is clearly subjective. Moreover, it can
change over time. A policy that began innocently may become entrenched as an intentional barrier to trade because the local beneficiaries
do not want to lose their advantage. Some examples of intentional and

unintentional barriers to agricultural trade are presented in Figure 2 and these are discussed below.

Figure 2: Forms of Interprovincial Barriers to Agricultural Trade

Type	Technical Impediments	Non-technical Impediments
Intentional Barriers	Cost-increasing Product Regulations	Monopolistic Product Marketing Agencies
Unintentional Barriers	Health, Safety & Consumer Information Regulations	Farm Support and Adjustment Measures

Technical impediments

Regulations in the food industry are necessary to protect public health and safety, but some product standards are used as an intentional method of protecting local producers. Provincial regulations governing dairy product substitutes are blatant examples of intentional barriers to trade. In Ontario and Quebec, margarine manufacturers are prohibited from colouring their product the same as butter. Ostensibly, this regulation was introduced to protect the local dairy industry, but it also affects the interprovincial movement of margarine. In other provinces, (e.g., Manitoba) margarine and butter are permitted to have the same colour, while in Saskatchewan and Nova Scotia, margarine-butter blends are allowed (Menzie, 1988). Consequently, margarine producers must operate different product runs and segregate their inventory depending on the provincial market. This interprovincial barrier adds to the costs of margarine right across the country, while offering a dubious benefit to Canadian dairy farmers.

There are numerous examples of cases in which product standards have been used to block trade. In Ontario, butter can be parchment wrapped, but in Quebec it must be foil wrapped. The need to organize a separate and more expensive packaging line for the Quebec market discourages the Ontario producers that are set up to serve their large local distribution network. Quebec's Language Law, Bill 101, is also cited as a barrier because French must be displayed more prominently on labels than English. Such labels are unlikely to be suitable outside Quebec which adds to the cost of shipping into the province (Trebilcock *et al.*). In addition to packaging material and labelling, container size regulations are also sometimes used intentionally to block interprovincial trade (Milne, 1987).

The need to adopt inefficient processes, such as the separation of production, packaging and inventory, was identified in half of the case studies on interprovincial trade barriers reported by Loizides and Grant (1992) (see Box 1). The loss in economies of scale because of these barriers leads to higher consumer costs, and the inability to develop a national marketing plan. Ultimately this also reduces the potential for Canadian food processors to compete in the international markets.

Inspection regulations and enforcement practices are other forms of technical impediments to interprovincial trade. At one time inspections were the principal means used to control interprovincial movements of milk. A dairy could not ship to the processor unless the provincial milk inspector had approved the farm. Of course, the inspectors were not allowed to cross the borders, which kept out the milk from other provinces. The licensing powers of the milk marketing boards make this barrier unnecessary now because each producer must have a provincial production quota.

The barriers to interprovincial trade created by some inspection regulations are entirely unintentional. Under the current regulations, products containing meat are limited to sale within provincial boundaries if the processing plant does not meet federal meat inspection standards. This applies to further processors of food products, as well as abattoirs. Consequently, a frozen pizza maker might only use meat from federally inspected plants, but not be allowed to sell in a neighbouring province because the pizza plant fails to meet federal meat inspection standards. The intent of the regulation is to maintain a high standard of health and consumer safety. The result, however, can be to unintentionally block interprovincial trade.

Box 1: Example of Agricultural Trade Barrier
Burns Food

Head Office:	Calgary, Alberta
Line of Business:	Food processing and distribution
Annual Sales:	$750 million
Main Markets:	Western Canada
Employment:	2,500 persons
Barrier:	Administrative practices, regulations
Source of Barrier:	Provincial governments, marketing boards

Description of the Barrier

Burns Foods has four operating divisions: a trucking company, a fruit and vegetable and grocery distribution company, a meat processing company and a fruit and vegetable processing company. The barriers facing them are as follows.

First, the barrier facing the trucking operation is lack of uniformity of regulations between provinces. For example, in Ontario the company cannot use 53-foot trailers, which are allowed in western Canada. Second, the fruit and vegetable distribution company cannot grow, for example, carrots in Alberta and ship them in bulk to Saskatchewan, Manitoba or British Columbia for further processing. The company can ship only packaged products. Third, the company has its main pork-processing plant in Manitoba. Its procurement of hogs is controlled by the hog marketing board of Manitoba. Fourth, there is inconsistency with regard to federal and provincial animal health inspection standards for processing plants.

Impact of the Barrier

Burns Foods would like to be able to use 53-foot trailers in Ontario as it does in western Canada, because it is more economical to do so.

The company would like to be able to ship domestically grown products in bulk to other provinces. If the company buys its hogs from Alberta, an agreement has to be reached between the Manitoba and Alberta hog marketing boards. The company regards the existing situation as a significant impediment to the competitive procurement of its major raw material input cost, which represents 80 percent of total costs. Pork processing is the major part of this company's business. The differences in animal health inspection standards mean extra administrative costs for the company in its efforts to ensure that it complies with different standards.

Overcoming the Barrier

In the case of meat processing, the company has no choice but to buy through the marketing boards. Although hog marketing boards don't have specific regulated quotas for supply management, the boards have such power that it is implicit in their operations to use a quota system to manipulate prices. Over the last two years, because of the different formula pricing by the marketing boards in Saskatchewan and Alberta, hog prices run between three and four dollars a hog less than through the marketing board system in Manitoba. The company hopes that the western provinces will get together and establish one marketing board to cover the industry and thus establish a level playing field in terms of domestic competition.

Source: Loizides and Grant, 1992.

The Canadian Agricultural Product Standards (CAPS) Act is another federal regulation that has become an unintentional barrier to interprovincial trade. Under the CAPS Act, all products crossing interprovincial or international borders must comply with the grading, packaging, labelling, etc. requirements of the Act, unless a bulk import exemption is granted. "The requirement of bulk import authorization frequently has a negative impact on the cost of procuring raw product since it reduces a firm's ability to obtain the closest, and often least expensive source of raw product" (Van Duren, 1992, p. 11). An example of this interprovincial trade problem is the Alberta-based fruit and vegetable company that cannot make bulk shipments of carrots for processing in British Columbia, Saskatchewan or Manitoba (Loizides and Grant, 1992).

Non-technical impediments

Most farm product marketing agencies have been given monopoly powers to control the sale of agricultural goods produced within their provincial boundaries, and to the first point of sale outside their province. These powers did not permit the marketing boards to limit interprovincial movements. The national supply management marketing boards (which operate for chickens, turkeys, eggs and milk) are permitted to regulate movements between the provinces through quota systems, under the National Farm Products Marketing Agencies Act (1971).

The importance of supply management as a barrier to interprovincial trade varies by province. The proportion of farm income derived from supply managed commodities is illustrated in Figure 3. Supply managed commodities account for 22 percent of total Canadian farm income, but in six of ten provinces (British Columbia, Ontario, Quebec, New Brunswick, Nova Scotia and Newfoundland), dairy and poultry products contribute over 30 percent of revenues.

Non-supply management marketing boards can also limit interprovincial trade and competition. For example, meat packers in Manitoba complain that they do not have free access to hogs in neighbouring provinces, but are forced to purchase their supplies through the provincial marketing board. This permits the Manitoba hog marketing agency (Manitoba Pork Inc.) to force up the prices paid by local packers by

Figure 3: Farm Income Derived from Supply Management Commodities

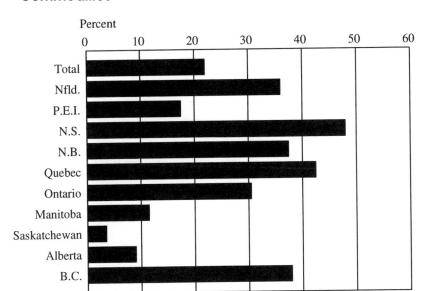

exporting live hogs. Arbitrage to eliminate these price distortions cannot occur (Loyns and Kraut, 1984).

Farm support and adjustment measures represent another form of non-technical interprovincial trade barrier. In most cases their effect on interprovincial trade is an unintentional, or incidental, effect of the program. Transportation subsidies are one type of support measure that has caused massive trade distortions. In western Canada the federal government has been contributing some $720 million annually to subsidize the transportation of grain and grain products to export ports (Thunder Bay, Churchill, Vancouver and Prince Rupert). This measure, which is often referred to as the "Crow Benefit," evolved from the 1897 Crow's Nest Pass Agreement with the Canadian Pacific Railroad (CPR). The purpose of the Agreement was to encourage agricultural settlement and to protect Canadian sovereignty through the construction of a rail line extension into southeastern British Columbia. The original Crow Rate applied to inbound settlers' effects, and the eastbound grain/flour movements from the points served by the CPR in 1897. As the CPR was expanded, and two additional railways were constructed, the differences in the freight rates at the old (1897) shipping points and the new shipping points created great inequity amongst producers. In 1925, the fixed freight rates on grain/by-product movements to export ports were made statutory at the 1897 level and were extended to cover all railways and shipping points. Eventually government support was required to sustain the railways at these below-cost freight rates. The subsidy was finally capped by the Western Grain Transportation Act (1982), but grain farmers insisted that the "Crow Benefit" should be paid directly to the railways.

After almost 100 years, federal involvement in the export movements of grain has caused a massive distortion of the Canadian farm economy and instigated countervailing interprovincial trade measures. Subsidizing grain exports inflates the price of feed, which discourages livestock production on the prairies. To offset this negative effect, the Province of Alberta began to pay a subsidy to their livestock producers to cover the higher cost of feed. The Province of Saskatchewan matched the Alberta "offset program" to defend their livestock feeding industry. In Manitoba, where the government decided against a battle with the Alberta treasury, the cattle feeding and processing industry has collapsed, and large numbers of feeder cattle are trucked to Alberta for finishing (Wilson and Hope, 1992).

These are only a few examples of interprovincial barriers to agricultural trade in Canada. Given the extensive literature on the subject (Menzie 1988, Veeman 1988, Clements and Carter 1984, Trebilcock *et al.* 1983, and, Haack, Hughes and Shapiro 1981), there seems to be little to be gained by further cataloguing, or by describing particular trade barriers. Therefore, the next section of this paper will examine the link between agricultural policy and interprovincial barriers to trade, before turning to the prospects for the elimination of these measures.

Agricultural policy and interprovincial barriers to trade

Official Canadian policy on measures that interfere with interprovincial trade has never been in doubt. As specified by the founders of the Canadian Confederation, in Section 121 of the Constitution Act (1867), "All articles of growth, produce or manufacture of any of the Provinces shall, from and after the Union, be admitted free into each of the other Provinces." Despite this apparent reference, in economic terms to free interprovincial trade, significant interprovincial trade barriers have been established.

In most instances, interprovincial trade barriers can be traced to industrial strategies that the provinces have used to try to maximize local employment and investment. Some examples are 1) the purchasing preferences given by provincial governments to local suppliers including discriminatory labour practices on public construction projects, 2) the requirements that breweries must locate plants in each province in order to gain access to the regulated distribution network and 3) the plethora of subsidies, tax holidays and other incentives used to attract manufacturing plants. Provincial industrial strategies may have also influenced the creation of some distortions to agricultural trade, but the most serious problems have resulted from the application of provincial and federal agricultural policy instruments.

The agricultural sector has demanded special attention by governments because of its inherently unstable nature. The incomes of farmers are subject to weather-related variability and to price cycles that farmers are powerless to change. Moreover, the rapid productivity improvement of the agricultural sector during the 20th century has created chronic labour redundancy and the low incomes that have come to characterize the plight of many farmers. These low and unstable incomes have led to a massive exodus of the farm population to the urban centres and demands for government assistance. The shrinkage of the farm population from 1951 to 1991 is presented in Figure 4.

Looking back, the technological and social changes in Canadian agriculture have been remarkable. In 1951, 20 percent of the Canadian population was located on farms; horses were still being replaced by gasoline powered tractors; rural electrification was incomplete; artificial chemical fertilizers and pesticides were limited in scope and distribution; and mixed farming was the predominant form of production. By 1971, half the farmers had left the industry and the farm population accounted for only seven percent of the total. This trend continued unabated, and by 1991 the farm population had been reduced to only three percent of the total.

Figure 4: Farm and Non-farm Population, 1951—1991

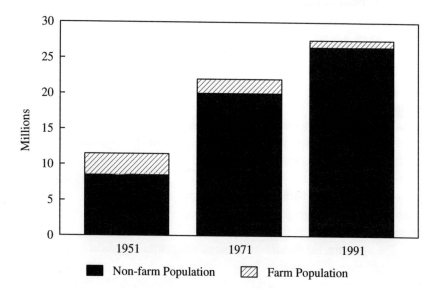

Between 1951 and 1991, three quarters of the farm population migrated to urban centres. The expansion of better paying urban jobs helped to facilitate the exodus from farming, but the chronically low and unstable incomes of farmers was exacerbated by the surge of low cost farm products resulting from rapid technological change. Governments responded to the problems of economic adjustment by instituting a variety of agricultural development programs, farm income supports and trade restrictions (MacFarlane and Fischer, 1968).

The 1964 Workshop of the Canadian Agricultural Economics Society (CAES) is one of the earliest forums to recognize the implications of government intervention for interprovincial trade.

> When a geographically large country such as Canada develops regional interests, as well as regional specialization in production, non-price barriers to interregional trade or subsidized interregional transportation become areas of sensitivity. (Trant 1964, p. 27)

Following Trant's analysis of agricultural development programs, Wood (1964) outlined the effects on interprovincial trade of farm income supports and marketing boards. The conference participants generally agreed that trade distortions were regrettable, but concluded that the benefits of these programs greatly exceeded these costs. For example, agricultural marketing boards were considered to have a negligible impact on interprovincial trade.

> It was felt that, although most marketing board legislation is enacted at the provincial level, hence potentially disturbing the competitive balance between producers in different provinces, *the actual distortions were not great in terms of social costs.* (CAES, 1964, p.67) [emphasis added]

This sanguine view of agricultural marketing boards was soon to lead to a significant expansion in their numbers and powers. In 1966 the Canadian Dairy Commission was established to administer the industrial milk subsidy, and by the early 1970s, coordination with the provincial milk marketing boards had evolved into the current national supply management system.

The logic that inspired supply management for the dairy industry encouraged its extension to other agricultural commodities. Following the passage of Bill C-176, the National Farm Products Marketing Agencies Act (1971), provincial marketing boards could organize national supply management systems. Under this enabling legislation, the Canadian Egg Marketing Agency began operations in 1973, the Canadian Turkey Marketing Agency in 1974, and the Canadian Chicken Marketing Agency in 1979.

Concerns about the effects of supply management on consumer prices were the subject of significant public debate (Food Prices Review Board, 1976), but little attention was given to their impact on interprovincial trade. The federal agricultural policy, set out in "A Food Strategy for Canada," (Whelan and Abbott, 1977) continued to emphasize income stabilization and support. Comments on trade were limited to assurances of "protection from short-term distortions in world commodity markets" and the negotiation of better access to foreign markets. Reference was made to the need to ensure competitiveness of the domestic processing/distribution sector, but the context suggests a distrust of the industry's behaviour, rather than any perception of problems with their operating environment.

Impacts

Without trade data it is difficult to quantify the impacts of interprovincial barriers on agricultural trade. Unlike international trade, there are no "customs" data collected on agricultural shipments between the provinces. Some estimates of commodity movements can be pieced together from secondary sources, but in general, the data lack sufficient precision to establish trends (Menzie 1983).

In the case of supply managed products, the interprovincial movements are based on artificial prices and the provincial production quotas that determine supply. At the time of their formation, each provincial marketing board received a "quota" share, determined in relation to their previous five year average production. As the Canadian population expanded, the principle of comparative advantage was supposed to be considered in the allocation of additional provincial quota. Veeman (1988) presents evidence that growth has been allocated according to the original entitlements (circa 1970). To the extent that the relative comparative advantage has changed, the benefits of free interprovincial trade have been lost for Canadians.

The costs of restricted interprovincial trade are magnified beyond the farm gate. The barriers to the free movement of raw commodities require the processing sector to operate smaller, less efficient plants. In addition, food manufacturers that use inputs like cheese or eggs in their products must pass on these costs in the form of higher prices to consumers (Consumers' Association of Canada, 1990). To the extent that the products of these Canadian food processors compete in international markets, or with import substitutes, the interprovincial barriers created by supply management affect their potential growth and profitability. "The savings to consumers from the elimination of interprovincial barriers and the reform of the supply management system could exceed one billion dollars annually." (Canadian Manufacturers' Association, 1991).

The agricultural commodities that are not covered by supply management (grains, red meats and horticulture) receive public funds through a variety of income support and stabilization programs. The total cost of subsidies and income transfers to Canadian agriculture are estimated to approach $12 billion annually (Gilson and Wilson, 1993). This is approximately equal to one-third of the current annual federal deficit in Canada.

Direct income transfers from consumers account for over 40 percent of farm support, while the remainder is received from government expenditures for freight subsidies, crop insurance, commodity-based "stabilization" programs, financial assistance and myriad services and grants. The federal government provides about two-thirds of total subsidy payments, with provincial governments contributing the rest. Such subsidy payments separate the prices received by farmers from their costs, and distort the signals of the economy that encourage farmers to shift their resources to the most efficient use.

Governments have also realized that their agricultural policies are often in conflict. Economic growth and development in the economy is encouraged by further processing thereby adding value to raw agricultural commodities. In some cases, farm income support programs encourage the export of raw agricultural commodities, or make these products more expensive to process locally than abroad.

Lastly, farm income supports can trigger retaliation. Within Canada some provinces have initiated subsidies to offset either the subsidies of other provinces or the distortions created by federal programs. Externally, Canada has been battling the imposition of countervailing duties from the U.S., whose producers claim Canadian farm programs subsidize exports to their market.

Politics of eliminating barriers to trade

At the beginning of the 1980s, public attention began to focus on the economic costs of regulation (Economic Council of Canada, 1981). The breadth and severity of provincially induced barriers to agricultural trade were identified by Menzie (1981) and by Haack, Hughes and Shapiro (1981). The awareness of these interprovincial trade barriers was part of a larger trend in the concern about non-tariff barriers to trade (Menzie and Prentice, 1983) and in the deregulation that was sweeping North America.

The number and severity of barriers to interprovincial trade created surprise and concern, if not despair.

> It is a lament that we have violated the principles implied in the economics of trade. At the international level, this departure from economic behaviour and general welfare principles is less pronounced than the damage we do to ourselves by violating the principles of general welfare in our own country. This is most obvious in the case of agriculture. We are in such a net of interventions imposed by federal and provincial governments that we don't even try any more to extricate ourselves. (J. J. Richter, as quoted in Menzie, 1983)

As Davey (1983) pointed out in his discussion of this comment, efforts to negotiate harmonized federal-provincial stabilization programs had been undertaken, and the federal Minister of Agriculture had announced that in future, all provincial stabilization and income assurance payments would be deducted from federal payments. But he too, was forced to admit that "Notwithstanding the recognition of the problem, there may well be increasing rather than less pressure towards the balkanization of the agricultural economy and greater barriers to interprovincial trade" (Davey, 1983, p. 129).

Political impetus was given to the problems of interprovincial barriers at the Regina meeting of First Ministers in 1985. The Ministers agreed to an initiative to examine barriers to interprovincial trade and to find ways to reduce, or eliminate, their effects. Subsequently, the 1986 meeting of the agriculture ministers confirmed the effort to eliminate barriers in a national strategy for agriculture. The ministers established a Federal-Provincial Agricultural Trade Policy Committee (FPATPC) which developed an inventory of interprovincial trade barriers. FPATPC also drew attention to the categories of technical and non-technical barriers to trade, and to differences in the requirements for their removal.

The signing of the Canada-U.S. Trade Agreement (FTA) in 1988 highlighted the importance of barriers to the interprovincial trade of agricultural products. Under FTA it could be easier to compete in the border markets of the U.S. than in neighbouring Canadian provinces. The commitment to reduce or eliminate interprovincial barriers was addressed directly in *Growing Together*, the federal government's "green paper" on agriculture policy.

We must also look carefully at our regulatory programs to avoid contradiction and to ensure that impediments to growth are minimized. Interprovincial trade barriers are of particular concern. . . . Within an era of increasingly liberalized international trade, foreign suppliers may enjoy greater freedom of access to Canadian markets than Canadian firms, due to the existence of interprovincial trade barriers. Canadian enterprises need to be assured that they will have at least equal access to domestic raw materials and markets as their foreign competitors (Agriculture Canada, 1989, p. 39).

The FTA created an urgency for the provincial governments to deal with policies and practices that hindered trade and fragmented the domestic market. On December 11, 1989, the federal and provincial Ministers responsible for Agriculture signed a Memorandum of Understanding (MOU) that confirmed their commitment to reduce interprovincial barriers. The expressed hope of the 1989 MOU was that increased interregional trade would improve the international competitiveness of the Canadian agri-food sector. It was hoped that productivity improvements encouraged by interprovincial competition could lead to import substitution and benefit all regions.

On July 4, 1991, the annual meeting of the ministers of agriculture produced agreement on a series of initiatives. A set of guidelines was developed for a "second generation" of supply management systems that would be more responsive to market conditions. Also, they agreed to the concept of a dispute-settlement mechanism to assist in the removal of technical barriers to trade (Economic Council of Canada, 1991).

Since 1991, some minor successes have been announced on the removal of technical barriers, such as for product testing for sulpha drugs in honey and the harmonization of potato grades, but progress in general has been moving at a glacial pace. At the same time, it has become apparent that one of the most controversial barriers may be resolved at a different level. Supply management requires import control to be effective. Consequently import quotas were introduced under Article XI to the General Agreement on Tariffs and Trade (GATT). However, and notwithstanding Canadian petitions, the GATT negotiators at the Uruguay Round have made it clear that Article XI will be changed. Without import control, the interprovincial barriers on supply managed commodities will also become untenable. Thus far, however, the Uruguay Round of GATT has yet to be completed.

The pace of change was also affected by the larger political effort to revise the Canadian constitution. A new "common-market clause" was proposed to address the shortcomings in sections 91 and 121 of the Constitution Act, 1867. This has generally been interpreted as only prohibiting the provinces from imposing tariffs on goods from another province. As a result, there is no clear authority to settle interprovincial trade disputes, or force the abolition of regulatory/administrative barriers to trade within the internal market.

The proposal for constitutional change would have broadened section 121 to deal with:

- barriers related to persons, goods, services and capital
- both tariff barriers and non-tariff barriers
- barriers created both by provinces and the federal government and
- barriers arising from legislation, regulations and administrative practices. (Government of Canada, 1992)

These changes were included in the Charlottetown Accord along with a host of other trade-offs and compromises that affected the division of constitutional powers in Canada. Of course reform of the Canadian constitution was defeated in a public referendum in October 1992, which effectively blocked the constitutional route to the elimination of interprovincial trade barriers—at least for the meantime.

Following the defeat of the Constitutional Referendum, the agricultural ministers met again (November, 1992) and endorsed a Memorandum of Understanding on procedures for the elimination or reduction of interprovincial barriers to trade. The 1992 MOU establishes a framework to eliminate or reduce barriers, an agreement on information exchange and consultation, and a description of the dispute settlement mechanism. Within the next five years, the ministers agreed to work towards the adoption of common national standards to remove technical barriers. The common standards are to be acceptable to the provincial governments, while taking international standards into consideration. The Ministers refrained from dealing with non-technical barriers in the 1992 MOU, because these measures are being considered under the Agri-food Policy Review.

FPATPC is identified as the monitoring agency for information exchange and consultation. The provinces have 20 working days to react to any new or revised legislation or proposed changes in regulations. In addition, the Ministers agree to consider the implications for interprovincial trade when contemplating changes in legislation or regulations. FPATPC is to conduct a review on the progress and necessary improvements for the annual Conference of Agriculture Ministers.

A dispute settlement mechanism is not defined in the 1992 MOU, but it is described. In the event that consultations between the provincial governments fail to yield a mutually satisfactory solution to an actual, or proposed, trade barrier, a dispute settlement mechanism is to be employed. The dispute settlement mechanism must be credible, transparent, effective, accessible, timely and public. On a separate level, the First Ministers have requested the Committee of Ministers on Internal Trade to develop a compliance mechanism. The ministers of agriculture agree to use it for dispute settlement, once approved by all governments.

The 1992 MOU moves a step closer to an effective means of dealing with the technical barriers to interprovincial trade. The lack of a dispute settlement mechanism means that the resolution of problems will remain difficult. The provinces have yet to agree on the format, the appeal procedures, or the method of enforcing the rulings.

The most recent development (July 1993) is the announcement of an internal trade secretariat, under the leadership of Mr. Art Mauro. The internal trade secretariat is charged with overseeing 13 teams of negotiators that will address a wide range of interprovincial trade barriers, including agriculture. The secretariat has been given a deadline of June 30, 1994 to produce a comprehensive internal trade agreement.

Prospects for change

It is easy to become sceptical about the prospects for eliminating interprovincial barriers to agricultural trade. After almost a decade of effort, the political process has delivered painfully little in the form of tangible change. Many of the regulations that cause problems occurred because individuals or groups in the private sector went to great administrative and political lengths to obtain protection from outside competition. These private sector interests who benefit from the barriers to interprovincial trade remain well entrenched. We might lament that these problems can never be resolved. Still, there are reasons for some optimism.

First, barriers to interprovincial trade in other sectors have been reduced. For example, the provinces have rescinded their requirements that breweries must maintain local plants in order to gain access to the provincial distribution system. This change resulted from international pressure through the GATT process and the realities of the FTA. A resolution of the current GATT negotiations could have a similar effect on the interprovincial trade of supply managed agricultural commodities.

Second, the provinces and the federal government are facing a fiscal crisis. Years of deficit spending to support, among other things, agricultural subsidies have created mounting debts and rising tax burdens. Something has to give, and income support programs, which have come to be viewed as wasteful, are high on the hit list. The recent announcement of draft legislation to finally change the method of paying the "Crow Benefit" to farmers may be an example of this new willingness to deal with long standing, contentious policy issues.

Third, the federal government seems determined to follow through with its efforts to reduce internal barriers to trade. This process is more fundamentally based than the particular party in power—it has become part of the bureaucratic mind-set. The regulatory review, which Agriculture Canada and other federal departments are going through, is evidence of the civil service's commitment to the removal of interprovincial trade barriers. With some notable exceptions, like the decision to reform the regulation of barley marketing, most of the action has been happening behind the scenes. However, the issues that have been identified in the regulatory review process will be the subject of ongoing negotiations during the coming year.

The reduction of interprovincial barriers to extraprovincial trucking is another example of federal commitment to freer internal trade. The federal government negotiated a change in the licensing procedures with the provinces, but it was very clear that they were ready to act unilaterally, if the provinces failed to cooperate. The federal government had the power to regulate extraprovincial trucking, based on a 1949 court case that clarified their constitutional authority.

The 1992 MOU of the ministers of agriculture to deal with technical barriers may suggest more than just federal-provincial cooperation. Section 121 of the 1867 Constitution has not been tested in the courts in relation to the full scope of federal power to ensure free trade within Canada. It is quite possible that the federal government is ready to test section 121, if necessary, and that the provinces recognize the likely outcome.

Finally, the political support from outside the farm sector for the removal of agricultural trade barriers is growing stronger. With less than 3 percent of the total population, farmers have lost much of their power to influence legislation. Canadians everywhere have been forced to adjust to deregulation, free trade and higher taxes. There is much less sympathy for the claims of farmers for special treatment, when everyone else has had to make comparable economic adjustments.

References

Agriculture Canada. *Growing Together*. Ottawa: Agriculture Canada Publication 5269/E, 1989.

Canadian Manufacturers' Association. *"Canada 1993" A Plan for the Creation of a Single Economic Market in Canada*. April 1991.

Clements, Douglas J. and Colin A. Carter. Nontariff Barriers to Interprovincial Trade in Swine. Winnipeg: University of Manitoba, Department of Agricultural Economics, Extension Bulletin 84-1, March 1984.

Consumers' Association of Canada. *The Reform of the Canadian Supply-Management System of Agricultural Commodities*. November 1990.

CMSMC. "Inter-provincial Transfers of MSQ at the Producer Level," Report of the CMSMC Sub-Committee, March 27, 1990. (Mimeo).

Davey, B. H. "Discussion" *Proceedings*. Edited by E.W. Tyrchniewicz. Vancouver: 1982 Annual Meeting of the Canadian Agricultural Economics Society, June 1983.

Economic Council of Canada. *Reforming Regulation*. Ottawa: Minister of Supply and Services, 1981.

_____. *A Joint Venture: The Economics of Constitutional Options*. Ottawa: Minister of Supply and Services, Twenty-Eighth Annual Review, 1991.

Food Prices Review Board. *Telling It Like It Is*. Ottawa: Final Report of the Food Prices Review Board, February, 1976.

Gilson, J. C. and A. G. Wilson. *Commercial Aspects of National Agricultural and Trade Polices for the Red Meat Industry in Western Canada*. Winnipeg: Manitoba Red Meat Forum, June 1993.

Government of Canada. *Canadian Federalism and Economic Union: Partnership for Prosperity*. Ottawa: Supply and Services, 1992,

Haack, R. E., D. R. Hughes and R. G. Shapiro. *The Splintered Market: Barriers to Interprovincial Trade in Canadian Agriculture*. Ottawa: Canadian Institute for Economic Policy, 1981.

Loizides, Stelkos and Michael Grant. *Barriers to Interprovincial Trade: Fifty Case Studies.* The Conference Board of Canada, April, 1992.

Loyns, R. M. A. and M. Kraut. *The Applicability of Electronic Trading Systems to Selected Farm and Food Products in Canada.* Winnipeg: University of Manitoba, Department of Agricultural Economics, Research Bulletin 84-1, April 1984.

MacFarlane, D. L. and L. A. Fischer. "Prospects for Trade Liberalization in Agriculture," *Trade Liberalization and Canadian Agriculture.* Toronto: University of Toronto Press, Private Planning Association of Canada, 1968.

Menzie, E. L. *Interprovincial Barriers to Trade in Agricultural Products.* Ottawa: Economic Working Paper, Agriculture Canada, 1981.

_____. "Free Interprovincial Trade or Provincial Self-Sufficiency in Agricultural Products," *Proceedings.* Edited by E.W. Tyrchniewicz, Vancouver: 1982 Annual Meeting of the Canadian Agricultural Economics Society, June 1983.

_____. "Harmonization of Farm Policy for Free Interprovincial Trade." *Canadian Journal of Agricultural Economics.* Vol. 36, No. 4, Part 1 (1988): 649-663.

Menzie, E. L. and Barry E. Prentice. *Barriers to Trade in Agricultural Products Between Canada and the United States.* Washington: IES-ERS, U.S. Dept. of Agriculture, April 1983.

Milne, William J. *Interprovincial Trade Barriers: A Survey and Assessment.* Purchasing Management Association of Canada, April 1987.

Trant, G. I. "The Implications of Interregional Competition in Canadian Agriculture for Federal and Provincial Development Programs." *Interregional Competition in Canadian Agriculture.* St. Anne de Bellevue, Quebec: Report of the Ninth Annual Workshop, Canadian Agricultural Economics Society, June 1964: 26-30.

Trebilcock, M., J. Whalley, C. Rogerson and I. Ness. Provincially induced trade barriers in Canada. In *Federalism and the Canadian Economic Union.* Edited by M. Trebilcock *et al.* Toronto: Ontario Economic Council and University of Toronto Press, 1983.

Van Duren, Erna. *The Impact of Technical Regulation in Canada's Agri-food Industry: Results of a Pilot Study with Horticultural Processors.*

Guelph: George Morris Centre, University of Guelph, March 1992.

Veeman, M. M. "Supply Management Systems: Impact on Interprovincial Trade." *Canadian Journal of Agricultural Economics.* Vol. 36, No. 4, Part 1 (1988): 711-723.

Whelan, E. F. and A. C. Abbott. *A Food Strategy For Canada.* Ottawa: Agriculture Canada and Consumer and Corporate Affairs Canada, 1977.

Wilson, A. G. and L. Hope. *Agricultural Support And Regulatory Programs which Impinge on the Canadian Livestock Industry: A Summary and Critique.* Winnipeg: Manitoba Red Meat Forum, March 1992.

Wood, A. W. "The Implications of Interregional Competition in Canadian Agriculture for Government Programs Aimed at Direct Support of Farm Incomes." *Interregional Competition in Canadian Agriculture.* St. Anne de Belleuve, Quebec: Report of the Ninth Annual Workshop, Canadian Agricultural Economics Society, June 1964: 31-50.

Federal-Provincial Communique. "Agriculture Ministers Move To Eliminate Technical Barriers To Trade And Competitiveness." Press Release, November 12, 1992.

The Balkanization of the Canadian Economy: A Legacy of Federal Policies

**Jean-Luc Migué,
École Nationale
d'administration Publique,
University of Québec**

GREAT CONCERN HAS RECENTLY BEEN EXPRESSED in Canada by politicians, bureaucrats and some economists over the tendency of provincial administrations to raise trade barriers within the national common market. Mostly they do so through a variety of budget and regulatory measures, including procurement practices, licensing requirements in the labour market and local content rules in the beer and wine industry. The federal government is commonly depicted as trying to reduce these trade barriers while the provinces stubbornly resist.

The proposition advanced in this paper is that numerous and important interprovincial distortions are caused by federal policies and that trade barriers erected by the provinces are in large part due to the activities of the federal government. Distorting practices by the provinces can endure mostly because the federal government acts as the enforcer of an interprovincial cartel, sterilizing the local economic cost imposed by provincial trade barriers. The idea that the federal government is a partner with the provinces in helping to sustain barriers to internal trade is not widely appreciated. This paper first describes the interprovincial distortions directly caused by federal policies. It then shows how the federal government acts as the enforcer of an interprovincial cartel in neutralizing the "federalist" forces of interprovincial competition.

Interprovincial resource mobility as the defining characteristic of federalism

Economic forces constrain the way governments may tax, regulate, and subsidize within a federation. The economic reality provincial governments must face is that, in ordinary circumstances, the costs of whatever policies they may follow cannot be shifted to people outside the province. The reason is that the price of goods, capital and labour is determined outside provincial economies. If, for example, a province wants to slap a comparatively high tax on capital, investment will leave the province and head for another province where the tax is lower and the return higher. Lower investment can lead to several sorts of unpleasant economic consequences, such as plant closures, unemployment, and slower economic growth. This is not true simply of taxes, but of regulations, and any other government actions which impose a cost on residents.

Because they can easily move away from unfavourable legislation by provinces, resource owners are sensitive to relative tax and regulatory actions of provincial administrations. Heavy taxes and strict regulations on productive provincial resources lead to high production costs in the province. The people who feel these costs the most can get their supply from outside sources or they can move their skills and their capital to neighbouring jurisdictions. By leaving the province they "vote with their feet." Not only do those who leave suffer, but those who stay behind inherit a higher-cost economy with less capital and fewer skilled people to make things run. Taxes and regulations of course can benefit a minority of people; those receiving subsidies and some industries protected from competition by regulations. It is the population as a whole however who bear this cost, even if many are never directly taxed (as is the case for the corporate income tax). And it is this majority that can place a brake on such policies.

The overall impact of internal free trade on provincial governments is toward reduced and more neutral taxes and regulations than would otherwise be the case. In conventional parlance, this is referred to as a better match between public services and the preferences of residents.[1] But such effects depend upon the free movement of resources. It is this that impoverishes a province where the government is given to inefficient policies. Free movement is responsible for the high "supply elasticity" (i.e. sensitivity to price) of goods, labour and capital in provincial economies that are open to the world and to other regions in the country. Under free trade, governments are forced to compete with each other in policy matters and cannot easily allow themselves to be inefficient. This process of intergovernmental competition under free trade is the defining characteristic of federalism. It operates in any political structure where political authorities have no power to tax or regulate the whole area where trade is free.[2] The end result is that decentralization forces governments to match services with variations in demand and in cost. Provincial and local taxes tend to become merely fees for provincial and local public services. In a country where resource mobility is unimpeded by trade barriers, taxes and regulations that do not meet this require-

---

1   The most recent if minor illustration of this process was the reversal of the Ontario government's decision to prohibit Sunday shopping. This turn around in favour of less regulation was clearly forced on the government by the freedom of consumers to get their supply from cross-border shopping. On this see Herbert Grubel and Gurmeet Khangura, "Cross-Border Shopping: The Role of Economic Forces and Government," *Fraser Forum Critical Issues Bulletin III*, The Fraser Institute, Vancouver, 1992.

2   This line of analysis is extended to the international level in J.-L. Migué, *Federalism and Free Trade*, Hobart Paper No. 122, Institute of Economic Affairs, London, May 1993.

ment become so costly to raise that they tend to be abandoned by provincial and local governments.

Distortions directly caused by federal policies

This "federalist logic" lets us take the next step and show that intervention by the central government reduces policy competition between the provinces. Because they cannot affect prices outside the province, provincial governments by themselves are in no position to shift the cost of their inefficient decisions to other members of the Canadian common market. This is of paramount importance for the current debate. It means that while provinces can inflict inefficiency costs on their residents, they are unable to affect interprovincial prices. It is in principle not valid to say that provinces balkanize the Canadian market. Because they have no choice but to assume the burden of their costly policy options, provinces are constantly facing constraints on their ability to distort prices and to balkanize the economy. The mobility of resources in a free common market makes it costly for them to pursue inefficient policies. The federal government has historically operated under looser constraints,[3] inasmuch as it possesses the power to rule over the entire economic union behind trade barriers. The federal government effectively can use its greater monopoly power over the national economy to erect interprovincial barriers. Its contribution to the balkanization of the Canadian economy outmatches the ability of the provinces to do so.

The federal government acts in two ways. First, through regulations, taxes and subsidies, it discourages economic agents from adjusting to local conditions. The federal government directly discourages competition between the provinces by raising some well-disguised trade barriers. These barriers reduce the mobility of resources and hence the pressures that individuals and firms may feel to adjust to changing conditions. It is these direct barriers put in place by the federal government that I want to examine before moving on, in the next section, to a

---

3   At least until the advent of the free trade agreement with the United States and Mexico.

discussion of indirect distortions caused by its influence on provincial administrations.

The distortions of interprovincial prices are a direct consequence of three categories of policies put in place by the federal government:

1) The central supply of non-public or divisible services
2) The partial subsidization of provincial services via equalization grants or cost-sharing arrangements[4]
3) The central regulation of economic and social behaviour across the Canadian common market.

In short, the federal government is player, even a major player, in balkanizing the Canadian economy. It is the source of regional hurdles to the movement of resources throughout the economic union. This of course goes against an idea widely held in Canada that only a strong central government can safeguard the Canadian economic union against the narrow protectionist forces of local and provincial interests. This view is understandable because the federal government does not impose explicit barriers such as interprovincial tariffs. Its barriers are more subtle.

To show that this is the case, it is important first to explain in more detail what balkanization is. A general definition of balkanization is the extent to which a public intervention dissociates the price of goods and services in a particular place (in this case a province) from their production cost and prevents normal adjustments to this distortion. This wedge between the price of services rendered and their cost discourages resources from moving to their most productive location in the country. For example, the price paid by residents of Regina or Fredericton for higher education services is only a fraction of their true cost. It is this sort of activity at which the federal government excels and to which we now turn in greater detail.

---

4   While still designated as shared-cost programs, federal transfers for health care and for post-secondary education bear little relation to the costs incurred by the provinces. Provincial governments can use the funds any way they like.

Interprovincial price distortions through central supply and central handouts

In a centralized regime such as Canada, certain monopolies and services are run by the central government. These activities of the central government can distort prices so that they no longer reflect costs. Among the most prominent categories of central provision are the supply of mail and port services, of public pension plans, of employment and training services including unemployment insurance, and even of rail and air transport services via state corporations. Less direct forms of central supply come in the form of grants to the provinces, among which should be listed all-purpose equalization payments to the provinces and cost-sharing arrangements in the field of post-secondary education, health care and social welfare.

A major tenet of central supply, and, one might say, of the Canadian ethic, is that public services should be provided equally to people no matter where they live. The little appreciated consequence of this is that, in making output more uniform across regions, it diminishes regional responsibility. More specifically, the centralized provision of public services acts as an implicit subsidy to producers and buyers in less developed provinces of the Canadian common market. Selling public services on the cheap to lower-income provinces has the same effect on producers in those provinces as subsidies to producers and exporters at the national level. The supply of below-cost pension or mail services in less well-off provinces reduce the production costs in those areas and encourage businesses and people to settle there preferentially, irrespective of their true profitably. Perhaps the major form of subsidy is unemployment insurance. Residents of regions with high rates of unemployment are taxed at the same federal rate as residents in regions with low unemployment. This means that a high unemployment region pays less than its fair (or actuarially sound) share of tax given its exposure to the risk of unemployment, and the low unemployment region pays more than its fair share. The fisheries in Newfoundland do not pay the true price of the workers they employ because the taxes these employers pay to the federal government do not reflect the cost of federal protection of these workers against unemployment.

More generally, in such an arrangement, prosperous provinces pay more than what it costs to supply their services, while residents of declining areas pay less than the production cost. Instead of reflecting regional demand and cost conditions as in a true federal system, the tax price of government services is higher (through federal proportional and progressive taxation) for people in upper-income provinces and lower for those in low-income areas.

In short, by assuring that every region gets the same level of service at different tax prices the federal government is discouraging the movement of resources to the place where they are valued most. This policy is a massive trade barrier. By reducing regional production costs in some parts of the country, it hinders the process of resource specialization and acts as a protectionist device in favour of lagging areas. By contrast, production costs are raised in the most productive provinces as a result of the increased tax burden. Overall the Canadian economy is balkanized.

Production subsidies, however, are only one side of the federal government's contribution to blocking trade. Consumption subsidies are also important. Our federal government subsidizes the local consumption of many services, such as higher education, health services, old age security, and welfare. It does so through equalization grants and cost-sharing agreements (officially known as Established Programs Financing).

Such equalizing programs lower the price of education or health services below their cost in some regions and raise the price above their cost elsewhere. For example, through its equalization and cost-sharing payments the federal government tries to guarantee a fairly uniform national level of higher education. Federal taxes being more than proportional to individual income, this means that residents of lower-income provinces carry less than the full cost of their education and health services, because a poor region pays proportionately less federal taxes, thus receiving a net inflow of federal dollars. The opposite holds for residents in more prosperous provinces. The benefits are higher than the cost for the residents of some provinces, lower for others.[5]

---

5   For a more systematic analysis of these centralist forces in the Canadian federal structure, see L. S. Wilson, "The Socialization of Medical Insurance in Canada," *Canadian Journal of Economics*, 18, May 1985, pp. 355-376. This view is in turn grounded in the more general theory of government size as

As a mechanism for redistributing wealth among regions of the country, federal distortions have potentially serious long-term effects. Federal policies that redistribute wealth among provinces reduce the concern that local economic agents would otherwise have to make necessary adjustments. Because of federal transfers, consumers and producers are discouraged from settling in those areas where their productivity is highest. Because provincial prices are dissociated from their costs, resources see no need to move from regions where they are less productive to regions where they are more productive. As this failure endures, the process of income growth is hindered in less prosperous regions. Far from doing away with provincial disparities, federal policies with strong regional effects amplify them by discouraging resources from moving to their most productive location.

In a true federalist structure, such violation of the true price-cost ratio across areas of a common market would cause the mobility process to be set in motion. Provincial authorities who dared to raise taxes above the value of services as perceived by their residents would soon find resources being repelled from their territory. Not so under the centralist arrangement in place in Canada. By virtue of the uniform tax regime implemented at the common-market level by the Canadian government, productive resources in prosperous areas have a reduced incentive to move away from jurisdictions burdened by their excess share (above 100 percent) of the common education or health programs. By the same token, producers in subsidized provinces are encouraged to stay in their less productive employment by what in effect has become an education and health cartel at the common-market level. Central handouts cause provincial or regional prices to be dissociated from regional costs. Equalizing government services at the common-market level is equivalent to cross-subsidizing regionally rather than at the industry level. Such subsidies to less developed areas inhibit the spe-

---

developed in A. H. Meltzer and S.F. Richard, "A Rational Theory of the Size of Government," *Journal of Political Economy*, 89, October 1981, pp. 914-927. The 1992 Ireland referendum campaign on Maastricht was almost entirely fought on that ground. The Irish were literally bought. It is estimated that Ireland stands to collect $ 12 billion worth of aid and special benefits from the European commitment to closing the "prosperity gap."

cialization of the Canadian community's resources and are protectionist in nature.[6]

In sum, the much debated procurement policies by the federal and provincial governments in Canada are just minor parts of a much larger distortionary process implied both in the setting up of a central monopoly and in the payment of handouts to provincial governments. This is not to deny that when the central government purchases its supply of a type of input in one region rather than another, even though it is more expensive, it is balkanizing the economy. By paying more than the minimum cost, it is offering transfers of wealth to some holders of regional factors, while imposing additional burdens on taxpayers/consumers in other provinces. It is then inhibiting the specialization of the community's resources; it is restricting trade. But procurement is only a small part of the picture. The outcome is no different when the practice is extended to all other public outputs directly or indirectly supplied by the federal government.

Handouts by Ottawa to investments and infrastructure in regions result in similar distortions. As part of the long-established Canadian regional policy, granting investment tax credits or subsidies to designated areas has one feature in common with direct subsidies to public services. These credits results in expenditures being made for the benefit of certain regional groups and at the expense of others, irrespective of their net profitability. Money injected in this fashion into the Eastern Quebec and Cap Breton projects are no doubt politically appealing, but have mostly served to slow down the inescapable decline of those regions. Viewed in this light, regional policies in effect cause regional prices to be dissociated from regional costs and thus result in the further balkanization of the Canadian common market. They are essentially a

---

6   Standardization by central supply or central handouts can be viewed as a situation whereby people in high-income and high-demand provinces are coerced into sharing their public services with people in low-demand regions. Standardization by central bureaucratic monopolies acts as a discriminatory tool by which the Canadian government collects part of the consumer surplus of high-demand buyers to transfer it to median income consumers.

trade barrier, as they change the interprovincial flow of capital, labour and goods.

Interprovincial price distortions through central regulation

The irony of the reigning centralist vision of Canada is that while the central provision of public services and the cost-sharing and regional-development policies in force may result in lower resource mobility and excess population in declining areas, social and economic regulations by the central authority lead to reduced investment and population in less prosperous provinces. The social charter, proposed by the federal government during its effort in 1992 to rewrite the constitution, was a step in the direction of entrenching rights to standardized health, education and social-insurance services, uniform environmental standards, and common union wages and working conditions (affirmative action programs). A possible, but unstated, consequence of the Charter would have been to cause production costs to rise throughout Canada. The ability of lower-income, lagging areas to compete with the most productive ones would accordingly have been reduced. Poorer regions would have been denied the power to compete with prosperous ones through lower wages, lower taxes or fewer environmental amenities. The demand for common standards come from interest groups in the most developed and prosperous urbanized regions of the country such as southern Ontario, the Montreal area and B.C. Union members and long-established plants in industrialized areas tend to support these initiatives. This is of course the reason many interest groups are keen to constrict the North American Free Trade agreement with environmental and labour regulations. Such regulations would keep Mexico from exploiting its competitive advantages.

Consider for instance the impact of imposing uniform affirmative action policies and collective bargaining rules throughout the Canadian common market. By raising labour costs by a larger percentage in lagging areas, these measures act as specific taxes on labour in less productive provinces. As labour becomes more expensive relative to capital, each unit of output produced in those regions is produced with less labour and more capital. But the inflow of capital is also reduced as the overall level of productive activity declines. In transforming regions of low labour productivity into high-cost areas, labour regulations can thus be seen as tariffs on the importation of capital into provinces that need it most. Similarly, extending common environmental standards to less developed provinces raises the cost of doing business in those locations and causes declines of capital inflow into those places, just like additional tariffs on capital imports. In a similar fashion, imposing standardized health and welfare services on all employers across the Canadian common market results in relatively higher costs in poorer areas.

The distortionary impact of the widespread regulation of entire economic sectors by the federal government should not be less evident than that of "social" regulations discussed above. They all hamper the regional specialization of resources. Among the most prominent categories of federal regulatory measures that act as interprovincial trade barriers, specific mention should be made of the fisheries and freight rate regulation, energy policies and exploration incentives, agricultural marketing boards, telecommunication regulations, the various conditions attached to business subsidies, and others.

Distortions indirectly caused by federal policies

The redistributive policies of the federal government foster resistance to necessary local adjustments in a second way. By releasing provinces from the consequences of their decisions, central subsidies and regulations encourage provincial governments themselves to show little concern for adopting adjustment policies. Equalization payments, established programs and central regulatory measures mostly serve to shield provincial administrations from the consequences of raising interprovincial barriers and raising the costs of production in their own province. These central actions reduce the pressures that provinces would otherwise feel to govern efficiently. Provincial governments in our federation have been able to indulge in distorting practices mostly because the federal authority has proven adept at shifting the cost of their policies to outside taxpayers or consumers and at neutralizing the federalist adjustment process. Indeed, the more inefficient the provinces are, the more they are compensated by the central authority.

Empirical measure of interprovincial barriers

The limited information available for the direct measurement of inter-provincial barriers is more in the nature of descriptive and qualitative evaluation than of quantification. In a study sponsored by the Ontario Economic Council in 1983, a number of analysts did provide an overall survey of the likely consequences of trade barriers but again with little in way of quantification. Trebilcock *et al*[7] conclude their assessment of provincially induced barriers to the mobility of goods, of persons and of capital with the statements that "their [interprovincial trade barriers] economic consequences remain difficult to quantify,"[8] and that "no data exist on how large an effect on the labour force these restrictions (on personal mobility) have."[9] On the other hand in listing and describing the various provincial policies, these authors provide a useful and comprehensive picture of the numerous provincial policies and prac-tices which restrict mobility. It is revealing that their overall assessment should conclude with the following statement: "In fact, it is difficult to predict that central or unitary governments will be less prone to distort internal trade flows than lower levels of government. The evidence presented in this book suggests the opposite."[10]

In the same collection of papers on interprovincial barriers to trade, Whalley[11] extends the analysis to an evaluation of both provincially and centrally imposed barriers to interprovincial flows of goods and factors.

---

7   Michael J. Trebilcock *et al.*, "Provincially Induced Barriers to Trade in Canada: a Survey," in Michael J. Trebilcock *et al.*, *Federalism and the Canadian Economic Union*, University of Toronto Press, Toronto, 1983, pp. 243-351.

8   *Ibid.*, p. 267.

9   *Ibid.*, p. 291.

10 *Ibid.*, p. 558.

11 John Whalley, "Induced Distortions of Interprovincial Activity: An Over-view of Issues" and "The Impact of Federal Policies on Interprovincial Activity," in Michael J. Trebilcock *et al.*, *Federalism and The Canadian Economic Union*, University of Toronto Press, Toronto, 1983, Ch. 4, pp. 161-200 and Ch. 5, pp. 201-242.

He also discusses the theoretical concept of distortion in terms of resource misallocation among provinces, as opposed to misallocation within provinces. Only policies that discriminate against one or more provinces are deemed to distort interprovincial flows. Only such policies are said to impede trade between Canadian regions. In suggesting that trade barriers imply dissociation of interprovincial prices from their costs, we have implicitly retained a similar concept of distortion. On the other hand we focused on the fact that provincially induced distortions impose a burden only on the residents of the implementing province. By contrast, when distortions between provinces are centrally induced, their cost is shifted to the Canadian economy as a whole by virtue of the fact that central regulatory and budget programs are implemented at the overall Canadian market level.

Whalley undertakes a survey of the most important interprovincial distortions imposed by both provincial and federal policies. His method consists in first evaluating the size of interprovincial trade flows in goods and services, in labour and in capital. By then assuming a likely range of distortion rates and provincial import elasticities, he concludes that "losses from interprovincial distortions of goods flows in Canada are small,"[12] ranging from less than one-fifth of 1 percent of GNP for 1974 to 1.5 per cent per year. "An annual welfare cost in the region of 0.06 per cent of the labour bill would result, an insignificant welfare cost."[13] As for distortions of capital flows, "an educated guess could be that the annual welfare costs are unlikely to exceed those for labour distortions."[14]

A more recent and limited attempt was made at measuring the costs of interprovincial trade barriers by the Canadian Manufacturers' Association[15] (Table 1). Procurement policies by Ottawa and the provinces

---

12 *Ibid.*, p. 192. Note that these numbers represent net losses, i.e. the algebraic sum of what consumers and taxpayers lose minus the gains realized by various interest groups from subsidies and regulation.

13 *Ibid.*, p. 193.

14 *Ibid.*, p. 193.

15 Todd Rutley, *Canada 1993: A Plan for the Creation of a Single Economic Market in Canada*, The Canadian Manufacturers' Association, Toronto, April 1991.

are assumed to have increased the costs of goods and services these governments purchase by 5 percent. It should be underlined that this figure includes the federal government's own purchases. These purchases make up 20 percent of all public purchases and systematically discriminate on the basis of regional criteria. Other barriers for which cost estimates are offered in the CMA study include those on beer and wine, which is said to amount to some $500 million in 1990 and, more importantly, agricultural barriers, which imposed a cost of some $1 billion in 1990. In these last two cases, provincial restrictions on trade within Canada could not long survive without support from the federal government in the form of quotas against foreign competition, nor without the organization of the national agricultural cartel by Ottawa. Our estimate is that roughly $2.5 billion in costs, or close to 40 percent of the barriers identified in the CMA study, are *directly* ascribable to exclusive action by the federal government.[16]

Table 1: Estimated Benefits From Single Market (in millions of dollars)

More efficient government goods procurement	$2,500
More efficient government services procurement	$2,500
Removal of trade barriers affecting beer and wine	$500
Removal of agricultural trade barriers	$1,000
Estimated Total Savings	$6,500

Source: Canadian Manufacturers' Association, *Canada 1993*, p. 4.

In contrast with the Whalley results quoted above, the gains realized by beneficiaries (mostly producers) are not subtracted from these numbers.

16   It is here assumed that 20 percent of public purchases of goods and services are made by the federal government. Interprovincial price distortions of agricultural goods and beer are entirely ascribed to the federal government on the basis of its unique power to close the Canadian market to foreign competitors. It is not without interest that this key role of the federal government in balkanizing Canada was not even alluded to in media reports, when the CMA study came out.

The CMA calculations focus on procurement practices and on the federal government's role as enforcer of the national cartel in two sectors: alcohol and agriculture. To realize that the federal government acts as the enforcer of the cartel of provincial agricultural marketing boards, simply imagine that the control of supply in the milk, egg and poultry sectors were left entirely to the provinces, with no quotas set by the federal government against imports of those products from abroad. Instead Canadian food processors would be competing in a single Canadian market and would remain free to purchase their supply from agricultural producers in the cheapest province. Agricultural supply management by the provinces in those conditions could not long be sustained.

The thrust of the analysis pursued in this paper is that distortionary procurement, of the type analyzed by the CMA, is just a part of the trade-barrier picture. The central government also discourages trade by dissociating provincial prices from costs in more fundamental ways. It does so through the central supply of uniform public services across the country, equalization and shared-cost payments to provinces and central regulation of entire sectors of the Canadian economy. It is these costs of which Table 2 tries to give us some impression.

The idea behind Table 2 is to measure roughly what government spending is likely to reduce the flow of trade in goods and factors. We can then speculate, based on this figure, how much Canadians may be suffering as a result of discouraged interprovincial trade. This table is not the result of a detailed and microscopic examination of spending programs. What it seeks to accomplish is first to provide a broad outline of federal expenditures depending on whether they are national or non-national in scope and impact. Our purpose is to identify federal fields of intervention that are of a national public-good nature and nondistortionary as opposed to expenditures that provide regional, local or private services. Actually we have separated out as non-distortionary seven government tasks where inter-regional spillover effects are most pronounced and as such they might call for central supply or some sort of national harmonization. These are defence, external affairs, immigration, Indian affairs, Veterans affairs, medical research, and science and technology.

Table 2: Federal Spending with or without Interprovincial Distortions (in millions of dollars)

	1960	1990
1. Expenditures in the nature of a national public good*	$1,677	$23,575
2. Distortionary expenditures	2,483	76,907
3. Total federal expenditures**	4,160	100,482
4. % distortionary (Line 2 as % of line 3)	59.7	76.5

*As explained in this paper, federal expenditures assumed to be of a public-good nature and nondistortionary include Medical Research Council, Defence, Immigration, Indian Affairs and Northern Development, External Affairs, Veterans Affairs, Industry, Science and Technology.
**Excluding public debt charges and the category "other."

Sources: Federal Expenditures for 1990: *The National Finances 1991*, Canadian Tax Foundation, 1992, Table 6.6, p. 6:11. Federal Expenditures for 1960: *The National Finances 1960-61*, Canadian Tax Foundation, Toronto, 1960, Table 1, p. 2 and Table 22, p. 36.

―――――――

Table 2 suggests that in 1990, in excess of three quarters of federal expenditures were regionally distortionary in nature ($76,907 million in Table 2). Included in this classification of distortionary spending are all federal programs which cause publicly-supplied services to be standardized across Canada, directly or through subsidies to provincial suppliers.[17] For in the absence of such homogenizing action by Ottawa,

―――――――

17   Federal transfers to the provinces (equalization payments, established programs, social assistance, tax transfers) represent approximately one quarter of the federal budget (when debt servicing is excluded) and they account for more than one quarter of the provinces' revenues. In the case of the Maritimes, federal transfers represent a quarter of their gross domestic product (GDP). Clearly grants to the provinces are of the utmost importance as a source of balkanization. At more than $1,200 per year per Canadian, these forms of assistance have an enormous impact on the choice of economic agents regarding their investment and their person. V. Dickson

some provinces would have offered more of those services to their residents, others less. By the analytical concept of balkanization, all such expenditures dissociate provincial prices from costs. They imply interprovincial transfers. They are made irrespective of their locational profitability and in that respect act as trade barriers in preventing capital and people from moving to their most productive location. Arbitrarily assuming, as the CMA study does, that these implicit distortions in regional prices imply a net loss of 5 percent to taxpayers and consumers, their cost would amount to some $3.8 billion in 1990. By comparison, the procurement budgets of the provincial governments amounted to some $80 billion, which implies a cost of $ 4.0 billion to taxpayers and consumers.[18]

Furthermore, our theoretical argument suggests that this quantitative measure of distortions originating in provincial budgets grossly exaggerates the provincial role in balkanizing the Canadian economy. Provincial governments cannot affect interprovincial prices. They are able to carry on their distorting practices mostly because the federal government applies itself to sterilizing the local economic cost of inefficient provincial and municipal policies. Inasmuch as the central provision of public services, as well as shared-cost programs and federal regulations, release provincial authorities from concern about the cost of their policy options, one can validly ascribe to the federal government a large share of the $80.0 billion in distortionary expenditures formally made by the provinces. The point is that federal budgets and regulations act as enforcers of implicit collusive agreements between the provinces.

Another significant result revealed in Table 2 is the trend in the magnitude of federal distortionary expenditures over the last thirty years. As a result of the increasing federal involvement in the direct or indirect supply of divisible public services, the share of its expenditures

---

and D. Murrel, "Is Atlantic Canada Becoming More Dependent on Federal Transfer?—A Comment," *Public Policy Analysis—Analyse de politiques*, 16, March 1990, p. 99.

18   The accounting above implies a loss both when the federal government transfers a dollar to a province and when the province spends a dollar on inefficient procurement. This procedure leads to some double counting, and the above estimates should be seen as upper bounds.

which can be classified as geographically distortionary has risen from less than 60 percent in 1960 to more than 76 percent in 1990. Considering that the public sector share in the economy has skyrocketed from less than 30 percent to some 47 percent of GNP, these results reveal a great deal about the negative effects of our overcentralized regime.

Distortionary interprovincial barriers as a measure of centralization

The analysis pursued above can help clarify a question which is hotly debated in academic and political circles in Canada. Conventional wisdom in our country has it that the Canadian governmental structure is overly decentralized, and increasingly so. Proponents of this view point out that the ratio of provincial and municipal spending to government spending has been rising since 1960. Table 3 shows that the share of federal spending in the public sector budget as a whole has declined from 50.5 percent in 1960 to 40.1 percent in 1990. This gives the very strong impression that the role of local and provincial governments has grown over the last three decades.

As a measure of centralization, these figures are misleading. Observed trends in federal and non-federal budgets are a poor indicator of the effective division of powers in Canada for two reasons. The first one is legal: the provinces were induced by centrally-devised financing arrangements into embarking on social programs which followed a national standard. Provinces have increased their expenditures in reaction to the incentives incorporated into national programs, such as cost sharing by the federal government. Provinces who would not take part in the movement were financially penalized. Over the years, several provinces, not only Quebec, have resisted the extension of federal activism into constitutionally provincial fields such as higher education, health and pension services, with little success.

Let us take a summary look at the sources of budget growth since the late '50s. A simple listing of the main initiatives proves quite revealing: hospital insurance (1958), technical and vocational training (1958), the Trans-Canada highway project (in the 1950s), the social assistance program (1967), post-secondary education (1967), health insurance (1968), regional policies in the 1960s and 1970s and the National Energy

Program of the 1970s and early 1980s. The aforementioned programs contributed most of the growth in public expenditures and they were all transformed into "national" programs at the initiative of the central government. To a large extent the budgets of the provinces were shaped by centrally-determined arrangements. None could afford politically to abstain from embarking on the programs. In this sense, then, changes in relative expenditures of provinces and the federal government are a poor measure of the degree of centralization in Canada.[19] It may therefore be argued that there have been effective if not formal constitutional changes in favour of centralisation in Canada in the last three decades.

Table 3: Total Government Expenditures, 1960 and 1990

	1960 ($ Millions)	1990 ($ Millions)
Federal*	$5,752	$125,081
Provincial and Municipal**	5,645	187,201
Total	11,380	312,172
% Federal	50.5	40.1

*Excluding grants made by the Federal to other Governments, to Hospitals and to CPP and QPP.
**Excluding Grants from Provincial Governments to Municipal Governments, to Hospitals and to CPP and QPP. Includes Expenditures of Provincial and Municipal Governments, as well as Expenditures by Hospitals and CPP and QPP.

Source: *The National Finances, 1991*, The Canadian Tax Foundation, Toronto, 1992, Table 3.13, p. 3:14.

---

19   By leading the movement towards nationally uniform programs the federal government ignored regional diversities and hence the requirements of true federalism. Most importantly it closed the exit outlet available to the Canadian population to remove their assets from the reach of unfavourable administrations. In the questionable hope of removing the wasteful duplication of functions, it sacrificed the benefits from competition between governments. Similar arguments have been advanced in the last half century in defence of central planning as a mechanism to economize on the transaction costs of markets; they are equally false.

The fatal weakness in measuring decentralization by observed trends in budgets is that the approach rests on a can-do-no-wrong view of government in general, and of central authorities in particular. It leaves unaddressed the problem of state monopoly and the attraction of centralism: a systematic bias in favour of more central power follows from the textbook depiction of central governments as entities concerned only with pursuing the common good. Once a central authority is perceived to embody the collective will, it is impossible to imagine that a federal structure is superior to a unitary regime. No analytical basis then exists for opposing central administrations entrusted with the task of supplying all public services, local, national and supra-national. Purely administrative decentralisation then suffices to satisfy the requirements of scale economies.[20]

Harmonization: a menace to federalism

Harmonization is defined as the action of converging toward similar tax structures, similar expenditure programs and identical regulatory rules, on the part of all government authorities in a common market. It is generally believed that harmonization is good because it reduces duplication of administrative levels. Duplication is alleged to add only to costs, not to services. This view rules out the benefits that can flow from allowing governments to compete with each other. In a market economy, multiple suppliers are considered desirable and necessary. Multiplicity generally implies a broadening of the range of choices. At least, the alleged benefits of harmonization should be weighed against the cost of increased monopoly power.

To understand the anti-competitive view of government most people favour, it helps to look at the two different perspectives on how governments work that solicit the allegiance of economists. The standard textbook assessment of the removal of trade barriers within national common markets concentrates on the distortions likely to ensue

---

20   For a more systematic discussion of this question, see H.G. Brennan and J. M. Buchanan, *The Power to Tax: Analytical Foundations of a Fiscal Constitution*, Cambridge and New York: Cambridge University Press, 1980, ch. 9.

from non-harmonized provincial tax and regulatory regimes. One school believes that provincial governments should not impose significantly different taxes because supply and demand in open economies are price elastic. Harmonization is alleged to be desirable because it makes it harder for taxpayers and regulated agents to avoid the displeasure of bearing the burden of these measures, by shifting their purchases, their savings and their persons to more clement provinces. Decentralized regimes allegedly induce economic distortions, because in their attempt to avoid unfavourable tax and regulatory treatment, citizens can shift their resources to less heavily taxed jurisdictions. Since the national common market confers more price elasticity on a large number of provincial economic activities, more coordination between provinces is called for. For instance, mobile members of the labour force are in a position to avoid provincial residence taxes, owners of capital are able to move away from investment taxes and consumers escape provincial sales taxes by buying from other provinces. Strong downward pressures are exerted on provincial sales taxes. In the orthodox, conventional perspective those consequences are undesirable.

It is striking that efficiency in this framework is seen as synonymous with maximum government revenue. The maximum revenue goal is standard among analysts of optimal taxation. It is most explicit in a recent paper, in which it is flatly stated that "the objective of each government is taken to be the maximisation of its tax revenue; all subsequent references to optimality and Pareto-efficiency are to be interpreted in that sense."[21]

In the more realistic view of governments as redistributors rather than producers of wealth, the overlapping of functions between levels of governments and its complement, harmonization, are to be avoided inasmuch as they serve as excuses for suppressing tax competition and for intruding into provincial responsibilities by the central authority. By contrast, a province that would dare to encroach on the jurisdiction of the central national authority (for instance by opening missions abroad) would be enhancing competition between governments. As the burden

---

21 R. Kanbur and M. Keen, *Jeux sans frontières: Tax Competition and Tax Coordination When Countries Differ in Size*, Discussion Paper No. 819, May 1991, Queen's University, Kingston, Canada, p. 8.

of such initiatives in an open provincial economy is assumed by the provincial population concerned, the initiative has the best chance of satisfying real preferences. If not, it is likely to be temporary in nature. On the other hand, centrally setting the priorities and goals of, say, provincial environment policies, or coordinating provincial agricultural marketing boards, do away with competition by removing any option the population might have had of moving to another region or of seeking a cheaper supply in a neighbouring province.

The truth is that policy harmonization does not require centrally coordinated action. When it serves the provincial community, harmonization between provincial programs, taxes and regulations occurs spontaneously through the competitive market pressures arising from the inter-regional mobility of resources. Through the invisible hand of inter-government competition, provincial levels of taxation and regulation tend to converge across the national common market, especially those affecting capital, the most mobile factor. Provincial and local taxes evolve towards taxing people in proportion to the benefits they receive. Harmonization is thus deplorable or desirable depending on whether it is imposed from the top by centralization or whether it proceeds from decentralized choices. The first version cartelizes the provinces, the second expresses freedom and competition. Duplication of a central government function by a provincial or local authority may prove beneficial; duplication of a regional function by the central authority threatens competition and is detrimental. Within the perspective of competitive federalism, coordination mechanisms have nothing to do with true federalism. They are even harmful to this system inasmuch as they are used to legitimize the cartelization of the provinces and to strengthen centralist tendencies.

In no way does this mean that the institutionalized participation of provincial or local regions in central policy determination should be condemned in a democratic system. It may well be one desirable element of the political decision-making process of the central government. But decision-making in this arrangement remains central in nature and as such goes against the federalist logic. Whether tax, budgetary or regulatory standardization results solely from the federal parliament, or from the interaction of central and provincial authorities, it still suppresses competition between governments as long as it applies uniformly to the entire Canadian common market. In the dichotomy of mechanisms assumed as instruments to reveal preferences for public goods, harmonization arrangements belong to the central voice process rather than the exit mechanism. And any measure which aids in harmonization, such as the balkanization of the internal economy, can have unfortunate consequences for economic prosperity.

Conclusion

This essay has argued that the federal government has been largely responsible for the interprovincial trade barriers we now find in place throughout the country. When a province puts up a barrier to protect some interest group such as farmers, or construction workers, it is doing itself harm. The provincial economy as a whole suffers, even if certain special interest groups benefit. But provinces would be less able to impoverish themselves in this way if they did not have the federal government to bail them out. Provincial politicians are sheltered in part from the consequences of making bad economic decisions because federal supply, transfers and regulations sterilize the cost of their decisions.

Without the federal government to shroud the effects of these bad provincial decisions, consumers could more easily get their supply from outside sources, while some voters would leave, taking with them their skills and their capital. This would result in lower provincial tax revenues, to the point where each province would provide its residents with services in line with the taxes its people pay. This policy competition is less likely in an economy where regional actions are neutralized in ways that cuts the link in each province between the government services people receive and the tax and regulatory cost of those services. Dissociation of the cost of a service from its value means that resources in the Canadian economy do not move to their most productive use. This dissociation, which largely is made possible by the federal government, is a major form of interprovincial trade barrier.

Interprovincial barriers may be costing Canadians billions a year in foregone economic opportunities. The exact measurement of this magnitude needs further research. The main impression I wish to leave the reader with is that interprovincial trade barriers come in subtle guises, and that the federal government's regulations, transfers and programs are largely responsible for the continued existence of such barriers.

Barriers to Interprovincial Labour Mobility

**Morley Gunderson, Director,
Centre for Industrial Relations
and Professor,
Dept. of Economics,
University of Toronto**

WHILE CANADA HAS OFTEN BEEN LABELLED a "nation of immigrants," the fact remains that interprovincial mobility is a much more important source of regional population growth than is immigration. Regional population growth from migration, for example, is about two-thirds attributable to interprovincial migration and one-third to international migration (Table 1). Such interprovincial mobility is a key ingredient not only for "nation building" but also for labour market policy and for our ultimate ability to compete internationally.

The dramatic changes that are occurring in the Canadian labour market are creating pressures to increase barriers to interprovincial labour mobility. An example is the bitter dispute between Ontario and

Table 1: Relative importance of domestic and international migration (1981-1986)

Province/ Territory	Total immigration	Numbers by source		% by source	
		Other provinces	Other countries	Other provinces	Other countries
CAN.	1,388,395	924,495	463,900	66.6	33.4
NFLD.	18,765	17,090	1,675	91.1	8.9
P.E.I.	10,370	9,480	890	91.4	8.6
N.S.	62,880	54,985	7,895	87.4	12.6
QUE.	139,350	66,915	72,435	48.0	52.0
ONT.	506,850	285,525	221,325	56.3	43.7
MAN.	75,995	56,680	19,315	74.6	25.4
SASK.	63,575	54,695	8,880	86.0	14.0
ALTA.	233,280	177,290	55,990	76.0	24.0
B.C.	221,290	151,680	69,610	68.5	31.5
YT.	4,900	4,620	280	94.3	5.7
N.W.T.	9,570	9,010	560	94.2	5.9

Source: Statistics Canada, *Mobility Status and Interprovincial Migration*, 1986 Census, No. 93-108, 1985.

Quebec over each other's preferential hiring practices for public sector projects.

Substantial adjustment is occurring in the Canadian labour market, emanating from such interrelated factors as global competition, free trade, technological change and industrial restructuring. In such circumstances, it is tempting for governments and interest groups to increase barriers to interprovincial labour mobility, in the hope of preserving jobs and incomes that are otherwise threatened by competitive pressures. This temptation is fostered by the growing importance of provincial governments and by the increased emphasis on decentralization. Unfortunately, these pressures to increase the barriers to interprovincial labour mobility are coming just at the time when there is also the greatest need to reduce such barriers.

The purpose of this paper is to analyze the barriers to interprovincial labour mobility in Canada. First, such barriers are documented, followed by a discussion of the growing need to reduce them. The determinants of interprovincial labour mobility are then analyzed, emphasising the role of artificial barriers to mobility. This is followed by a discussion of the effects of interprovincial labour mobility and hence of the implications of reducing such barriers. The paper concludes with a summary and some observations on the importance of reducing the barriers to interprovincial labour mobility.

Barriers to interprovincial labour mobility[1]

In analyzing the barriers to interprovincial labour mobility, it is important to make a distinction between natural, economic barriers and artificial barriers imposed by law and regulation, although sometimes the distinction is blurred. Distance, and cultural and language differences, are natural economic barriers to mobility, although the language differences can be affected by laws and regulations. The artificial barriers that are the subject of this chapter include professional occupational licensing, government occupational licensing of trades, preferential hiring practices, income security programs, education and language requirements, and employment standards legislation. These artificial barriers to mobility are the proper subject of policy analysis precisely because they are subject to policy control.

Professional occupational licensing and certification

Self-governing professions are usually given the power to set standards with respect to who practices in that profession. Some, like medicine and law, determine who has the exclusive "right to practice" (occupa-

---

1   More detailed documentation of these barriers is contained in Economic Council of Canada (1991b), Employment and Immigration Canada (1979), Muzondo and Pazderka (1979), Revay and Associates (1992), Smith, Gunther and Associates (1992), Trebilcock, Kaiser and Prichard (1977), and Trebilcock, Whalley, Rogerson and Ness (1985).

tional licensing) while others have a more limited power to determine who receives the "exclusive right to title" by being given a particular certification (occupational certification), even though others can do the work without the certification.

The professions themselves are given this power because they are assumed to have the information to determine minimal quality standards in order to "protect the public," usually done in situations where the general public cannot be expected to have enough information to evaluate the quality of the service, they are infrequent users, and the effects of a bad decision can be severe. The problem, of course, is that the professions may have an incentive to restrict entry so as to artificially sustain salaries—a problem that is particularly severe because they can also influence the demand for their services.

Interprovincial mobility in the professions is inhibited by a variety of aspects pertaining to occupational licensing and certification. Different requirements with respect to such factors as education, "intern" training, licensing examinations, and even provincial residency periods can make it costly for migrants to "re-qualify," especially when there is a lack of reciprocity across provinces. As indicated by Trebilcock, Whalley, Rogerson and Ness (1983, p. 273) "Out-of-province transfers are commonly subject to standard admissions criteria which impose upon experienced professionals the requirement of completing licensing courses and examinations and redoing their apprenticeships regardless of their experience. Often an arbitrary number of years of practice is made a pre-requisite to seeking a licence."

An example of a seemingly arbitrary restrictions on a profession (and there are many more in this vein) are the restrictions that certain accountants face. In about half the provinces certified general accountants can audit the books of publicly traded companies. In the other provinces only chartered accountants can do this. One Quebec accountant complained that "I lost clients who went and set up businesses in Ontario where we have no audit rights so we couldn't continue to serve the client" (Alan Swift, CP wire service, July 28, 1993). Ironically, as part of the Free Trade Agreement between Canada and the United States, chartered accountants and certified accountants have equal rights in both countries.

In spite of the strong self-regulatory aspect of the professions, governments can also impose their will. In the summer of 1993 the Ontario government declared its intention to reign in medical costs by refusing to license new doctors educated outside the province. This is an example of how a desperate government looking for an easy solution to fiscal problems can use its power over licensing to block labour mobility.

Government licensing and certification of trades

Licensing and certification may also be done by different levels of government usually for particular trades or occupational groups such as electricians, plumbers or hairdressers. Almost one-third of the craftworkers in production jobs are licensed. The province of Ontario, for example, licences some 33 trades, and has delegated the power to municipalities to licence more than 60 others (Trebilcock, Kaiser and Prichard, 1979, p. 118).

Interprovincial mobility is restricted by lack of uniformity both in the requirements for the licence and in the types of trade that are licensed. As well, there is a lack of full reciprocity in recognizing qualifications from other provinces. Residency requirements and even higher fees are occasionally imposed on non-residents.

A substantial degree of uniformity has been obtained through the voluntary Red Seal or interprovincial standards program co-ordinated by Employment and Immigration Canada. Reciprocity is obtained through the "mutual recognition" of qualifications across participating provinces for tradespeople who have passed a common exam. The program is generally recognized as a successful vehicle for harmonization of standards in this important area, and it has been labelled a "model of flexibility and cooperation" (Watson, 1983). However, it is not universal, since not all trades are covered across all provinces. And one may question of how much use uniformity is when provincial governments give preference to hiring workers from their own province, as the next section describes.

Preferential hiring

In the public sector, governments often give preference to the hiring of local residents as public employees. Also, preferential procurement practices in their contracting process may apply to services as well as goods, thereby affecting mobility both directly and indirectly. Todd Rutley (1991) of the Canadian Manufacturer's Association estimates that preferential procurement costs residents of the province being "protected" roughly $5 billion a year more than they would pay if government simply bought its goods and services from the cheapest suppliers.

Preferential hiring practices may be the biggest of all barriers between the provinces. The main disputes are between Ontario and Quebec, and the Maritimes and Quebec. Quebec has rules which encourage municipalities to buy buses from Novabus of St-Eustache over buses from Ontario Bus Industries, and New Flier Industries of Winnipeg. Quebec is almost closed to contractors and manufacturers of building material who do not have their principal place of business in the province. This cuts Ontario contractors out of the roughly $14 billion a year Quebec market. In the summer of 1993, Ontario "retaliated" cutting Quebec contractors out of about $8 billion of Ontario government public works spending, and by discouraging Ontario communities from buying Quebec-made buses (*Globe and Mail*, September 28 1993, pp. B1-B2).

Governments have also imposed preferential hiring practices in the *private* sector, especially through the granting of permits for natural resource projects or construction. Examples include: federal pipeline projects; the Newfoundland oil and gas industry; mineral exploration permits in Quebec; and Northern Development projects in Saskatchewan. As indicated in Milne (1987, p. 4):

> Newfoundland has a registry of workers giving Newfoundlanders first preference on jobs associated with petroleum and gas exploration. Quebec gives preference to Quebec labourers and mining engineers when issuing mineral exploration permits. A northern preference hiring clause in lease agreements in Saskatchewan requires that 50 per cent of the staff be residents of Northern Saskatchewan. In Alberta, all projects requiring Industrial Development Permits, Forest Management Agreements or Coal Development Permits must give preference to Alberta labourers. In both Quebec and Nova Scotia public ser-

vice legislation gives preference in recruiting to their own residents.

Legislation in the Quebec construction industry requires that employers provide preferential hiring on the bases of a combination of annual hours worked and region of residence. With respect to the regional dimension, preferential hiring is given to local employees, then to employees from outside the region, with out-of-province employees not being allowed to work at all unless no employees are available from within the province.

Unions that act as hiring halls, mainly in the construction industry, also give preferential treatment to local members. This can apply to workers under the Interprovincial Red Seal program as well. While this preferential hiring under the hiring hall can deter mobility, it is also the case that the hiring hall can enhance mobility by providing information on jobs available elsewhere.

Income security programs

While providing important income support, income security programs can also deter mobility through a variety of mechanisms such as residency requirements, limits on portability and differences in benefits. They can also affect mobility, however, by providing the income support that enables some people to be able to afford not to move, and others to cover the cost of a move.

Unemployment insurance can discourage mobility out of high unemployment regions, especially when regionally extended benefits are involved. Although formal residency requirements do not exist because it is a federal program, people who move may lose their eligibility if the move is interpreted as making them less available for work.

While welfare is under provincial jurisdiction, the federal cost sharing arrangements prohibit requirements with respect to periods of residency. Administrative practices, however, may give preferences to residents, especially when administered by municipalities. This can also be the case with respect to eligibility for subsidies or assistance in such areas as housing, senior citizens lodgings, health care or prescription plans.

Sometimes welfare programs can actually promote mobility. In the summer of 1993 the newly elected conservative Alberta government reduced certain welfare payments. Since then roughly 1,000 welfare recipients have been moving to British Columbia each month to partake of welfare payments which they believe to be more generous. Such mobility is of questionable value as the incentives driving people to move have nothing to do with how productive they will be in the new workplace, if work is ever found.

Public pension plans, namely the Canada and Quebec Pension Plans, are portable, so they do not restrict mobility. Private occupational pension plans, however, can deter mobility by not being fully vested, in which case an employee losses the employer's contribution upon leaving. As well, the employer's and the employee's contribution may be "locked-in" until the normal retirement age, if the employee leaves prior to that age. Transferability of full pension benefits is usually limited to reciprocal arrangements amongst certain employers or in multi-employer collective agreements. While such a lack of portability can deter mobility, this must be traded off against any positive effects on deterring unwanted turnover.

Education system and language

Barriers to the interprovincial mobility of labour may also exist through the education system. At the elementary and secondary school level, parents may be inhibited from moving because non-standardized curriculum or testing means that students may not be given full credit for education elsewhere. Differences in the grade levels required for graduation from high school may also create complications.

At the university level, mobility across provinces may be deterred by implicit or explicit quotas, especially in certain professional areas, as well as by reduced access to financial assistance.

Quebec's language legislation under Bill 101 may deter mobility into that province by requiring that education and other services be in French. Similarly, the unavailability of education or other services in French outside Quebec may deter mobility out of that province.

Employment standards

Since labour issues are under provincial jurisdiction, considerable differences can and do exist across the provinces with respect to various labour standards policies: minimum wages; hours of work and over-time; layoffs and dismissals; human rights and anti-discrimination; occupational health and safety; and workers' compensation. Some at-tempts have been made at standardization or harmonization, especially in the occupational health and safety area (e.g., the Workplace Hazard-ous Materials Information System—WHMIS). In general, however, there is substantial variation, just as there is with respect to collective bargaining laws.

Such legislation may be an important determinant of business location and investment decisions, and the lack of harmonization may pose significant costs for employers doing business in different jurisdic-tions. However, its direct effect on labour mobility itself is not likely to be substantial.

Growing importance of reducing barriers

The same competitive forces (e.g. global competition, free trade, indus-trial restructuring, technological change) that are increasing the political pressure to erect further barriers to interprovincial labour mobility (largely to preserve jobs) also increase the importance of reducing such barriers so as to achieve the restructuring, specialization and economies of scale that are necessary to create a strong, competitive domestic economy. In essence, a strong internal market is necessary to compete in external markets. The importance of internal labour mobility is enhanced by the fact that the competitive pressures are creating adjust-ment problems on both the "upside" (e.g. skill shortages, job vacancies, retraining needs) as well as the "downside" (e.g. plant closures, perma-nent job losses, mass layoffs). Labour mobility can ease the adjustment by facilitating the reallocation of labour from declining sectors to ex-panding sectors. This in turn can reduce unemployment as well as the structural bottlenecks that inhibit efficiency and the ability to rapidly move into new market opportunities.

By reducing such structural bottlenecks, and by facilitating the reallocation of labour from sectors of low productivity to sectors of high productivity, labour mobility is also a key ingredient of productivity growth. Such productivity growth in turn is increasingly necessary for international competitiveness. This connection between labour productivity and competitiveness has been emphasised in a variety of ways. First, relatively high wage countries like Canada must compete on the basis of a high-productivity, high value-added strategy rather than on the basis of low wages, given that labour costs in countries like Mexico, Taiwan, Korea, Hong Kong and Brazil, tend to be 15 to 20 per of those in Canada.[2] Second, the competitiveness of developed nations like Canada depends less on conventional factors like natural resources, physical capital, financial capital, access to markets, and even technology and innovation—all of which are now increasingly available on an international basis and easily diffused. Competitiveness depends more on developing market niches based on quality and service—factors that are heavily influenced by the effective utilization of our human resources. Third, Canada's international competitiveness, especially since the early 1980s, has increasingly been threatened by our poor productivity performance—the worst of the G-7—especially relative to our major trading partner, the United States.[3] These factors suggest that productivity is increasingly a key ingredient in competitiveness and the sustaining of high wages and good jobs. Reducing barriers to interprovincial labour mobility in turn is a key ingredient to enhancing labour productivity by facilitating the efficient allocation of labour to its most valued use.

Labour mobility is also a key ingredient of a positive adjustment strategy, in the direction of basic market forces, rather than away from them. Canadian labour market adjustment programs, especially unemployment insurance, have traditionally emphasised income maintenance rather than retraining or mobility.[4] While providing important

---

2   Canada's changing international position with respect to labour cost is discussed in Gunderson and Verma (1992).

3   Prosperity Secretariat (1992, p. 9). The other G-7 countries are Japan, Germany, France, Italy and the United Kingdom.

4   Of the seven major industrialized nations (United States, Canada, the United Kingdom, West Germany, France, Sweden and Japan) Canada ranks lowest in terms of the per cent of its public expenditures that are spent on active adjustment programs like training, and highest in terms of income maintenance programs like unemployment insurance (Economic Council of Canada, 1991a, p. 131).

income support, such income maintenance programs can encourage the retention of labour in declining sectors and regions. In the terminology used by Trebilcock, Chandler and Howse (1990, p. 123), they encourage the "stay" rather than "exit" option of adjustment. In contrast, programs like retraining and mobility facilitate the reallocation of labour from declining to expanding sectors and regions, and thereby encourage adjustment in the direction of basic market forces. Such continuous mobility is particularly appealing because it involves marginal adjustments which, if consistently followed, reduce the need for inframarginal adjustments which are likely to be more disruptive.

The importance of internal labour mobility is brought to the fore by international developments, especially in the European Economic Community (EC). In spite of the tremendous cultural, social and political differences that prevail across the countries of the EC, there is the realization that the free flow of labour between them is as important to competitiveness as is the free flow of capital and goods. As such, the Single European Act of 1986 was to eliminate barriers to the free flow of labour as well as of capital, trade and services between member states by 1992. The elimination of barriers to labour mobility involved such procedures as the "mutual recognition" of educational and occupational licensing requirements (Springer, 1992; Thom, 1992). The ability of countries like Canada to compete and bargain with such emerging trading blocs also requires the elimination of barriers to efficient labour mobility. Surely what the EC is doing *across* countries is an attainable goal *within* Canada.

The importance of reducing artificial barriers to labour mobility is fostered by the growing realization that regulations ostensibly designed to "protect the public interest" often protect those who are regulated, as they "capture" the benefits of regulation.

In summary, the reduction of barriers to interprovincial labour mobility has been increasingly emphasised for a variety of reasons: to deal with both the downside and upside adjustment problems that are increasingly affecting our labour markets; to ensure that the productivity of our labour does not slip and so jeopardize our international competitiveness and the ability to sustain high-wage jobs; to foster labour mobility as a key ingredient of positive adjustment in the direction of basic market forces and to reduce the necessity of disruptive inframarginal adjustments; to meet the competitive challenges posed by the free flow of labour within the EC; and to achieve the benefits of deregulation in general.

Determinants of internal labour mobility: theory and evidence

Conventional economic analysis of the determinants of internal geographic labour market mobility regards such mobility as a human capital investment decision, determined by the costs and benefits of such decisions. The labour market benefits are the wages and job opportunities. The costs include those involved in acquiring information about the move as well as in making the move itself. Geographic mobility associated with labour market moves is also intricately tied to other decisions about such factors as housing, language, schooling, family ties, taxes and transfers, and so it is affected by the costs and benefits associated with these factors. Geographic labour mobility is usually a family decision and hence is further complicated by the current dominance of the two-earner family.

The empirical evidence[5] on the determinants of geographic labour market mobility generally confirms the predictions of economic theory. That is, mobility occurs from low wage, high unemployment regions to higher wage, low unemployment regions, and it is negatively affected by the distance and other costs of the move. Mobility is much higher for younger people because of the longer benefit period over which they can amortize the costs, as well as the lower costs associated with fewer disrupted family ties, and lower forgone income if they leave a job, and less likelihood of loosing seniority or pension benefits. The Atlantic and Prairie provinces are the main sources of out-migration, while Ontario and British Columbia are the main destinations. Mobility into and out

---

5   Canadian studies include Courchene (1970, 1974), Grant and Vanderkamp (1976), Laber and Chase (1971), Mansell and Copithorne (1986), McInnis (1970), Osberg and Gordon (1991), Robinson and Tomes (1982), Shaw (1985), Vanderkamp (1968, 1971, 1972, 1976, and 1986) and Winer and Gauthier (1982).

of Quebec is lower than for most provinces, reflecting linguistic and cultural differences.

What effect do the sorts of trade barriers discussed here have on labour mobility? There is some evidence that transfer payments, especially those with a regional component (e.g., regionally extended unemployment insurance and regional equalization payments) slow down the process of internal migration (Courchene 1970; Economic Council of Canada 1991b; Shaw 1985; Winer and Gauthier 1982).

The Economic Council of Canada (1991b, p. 43) provides evidence indicating that the conventional net *out*migration that characterized the Atlantic provinces in the 1960 was reversed, becoming net *in*migration in three of the four provinces after the 1971 liberalization of unemployment insurance.

Winer and Gauthier (1982) indicate that the effect of UI on mobility is sensitive to how the relationship is specified in the empirical procedure. Osberg and Gordon (1991) discuss this ambiguity in the empirical literature. Their own results, prepared for the ministry of Employment and Immigration indicate that unemployment insurance does not usually have a statistically significant impact on migration. They also find inter-industry mobility to be more prominent than inter-regional mobility.

While there is a considerable empirical literature indicating that occupational licensing enhances the income of those who are licensed, there is less evidence on the effect of licensing on regional mobility. The limited evidence that exists, based on U.S. data, indicates that occupational licensing reduces geographic mobility (Kleiner, Gay and Greene 1982; Pashigian 1979, 1980).

Impact of regional labour mobility

Labour mobility, like all market adjustments, clearly creates winners and losers. Those who make the moves are clearly gainers—that is why they move in the first place. Some mistakes will be made and some moves will only be temporary—which is why there is a substantial degree of return migration. However, on net, the movers are better off as a result of the mobility.

The consequences of mobility are somewhat more complicated for people in the receiving region as well as non-movers in the sending region. By fostering mobility from low wage, high unemployment regions, to high wage, low unemployment regions, regional labour mobility should reduce the wage and unemployment differentials that induced the mobility in the first place. This tendency towards convergence or factor price equalization implies that there will be some losers in the host or recipient region whose wages will be lowered by the influx of substitute labour. These groups will tend to support the barriers that otherwise discourage such mobility. On net, however, the recipient region gains because of the more efficient utilization of labour associated with the mobility. Non-movers in the sending region should also gain because the outward migration should reduce unemployment as well as downward pressure on wages. In essence, migration is a positive sum game, with the economic welfare of the country enhanced by the more efficient allocation of labour. These efficiency gains also provide the means to compensate the losers, for example through the retraining of those who may lose their jobs because of inmigration.

These consequences of regional labour mobility are complicated by a number of other factors. In situations where a provincial government subsidizes education or training, there may be a "brain drain" problem if these people systematically move to other regions. This is not a problem if the individuals themselves had paid for their education or training, since they would then simply be appropriating the market returns to their human capital investment. The problem arises if the state pays for some of the investment and then loses the return because of the geographic mobility of the individual.

Problems may also arise if mobility is induced by natural resource rents that enable certain regions, for example, to provide more public services *and* lower taxes.[6] Such fiscally induced migration may lead to more in-migration than would otherwise be prompted by wage and unemployment rate differentials and labour market efficiency considerations alone. This may "depress" wages in the receiving region, given the surplus of labour that has entered for reasons other than labour market considerations. The long-run, general equilibrium properties of

---

6   Such mobility is discussed in Boadway (1992), Winer and Gauthier (1982) and Osberg and Gordon (1991) in the Canadian context, especially as a rationale for equalization grants to certain provinces.

this type of mobility, however, are difficult to establish. It is not clear, for example, that this is any different than mobility that is induced by any other non-labour market consideration such as climate or cultural ties. If this leads to low "compensating wages" being paid because of these other amenities, then this should also prompt an influx of business to take advantage of the lower wages and readily available supply of labour. This, in turn, should increase wages and reduce unemployment. The final equilibrium will reflect a trade-off of wages and employment probabilities against a variety of amenities (and disamenities) that exist inside and outside the labour market, reflecting the fact that mobility occurs for reasons other than labour market considerations, and such mobility is driven by total utility and not just wage and employment considerations.

Sociological perspectives also often offer a different view of the efficiency of geographic labour mobility. Myrdal, for example, emphasised that outmigration typically involves the most skilled and able young persons. This reduces the growth possibility of the region, leading to further exodus. In essence, "decline begets decline" and a vicious circle forms. This is in contrast to the economic perspective that would emphasise that the most able are also the most highly paid, and that the out-migration should raise wages of the "stayers" by reducing excess supplies of labour that otherwise depress wages.

The new neoclassical growth theory (e.g., Lucas, 1988; Romer, 1986, 1990) also offers a potentially different view of the efficiency of migration, although the policy implications of that perspective have not yet been fully developed and it has not formally been applied to the migration issue. According to that perspective, growth does not diminish as labour flows in because the process of growth generates benefits beyond those accruing to the person who has moved. These general benefits are called "externalities."

In essence "growth begets further growth." The higher productivity associated with the externalities and the interactions of migration to growth centres can lead to polarization rather than convergence. Migration is still efficient—in fact, it fosters the externalities and interactions—but it can lead to increasing inequality, rather than a convergence of income across regions.

Clearly, theoretical considerations suggest that the expected impact of regional labour mobility on the income of persons in the receiving region as well as on the income of "stayers" in the sending region is not a straightforward matter. Empirical evidence, however, suggests that such mobility within a country tends to reduce the income and unemployment rate differences that gave rise to the mobility in the first place. This is the case in many of the Canadian studies on the determinants of migration cited earlier.[7]

The equalizing effect of regional mobility is perhaps most starkly illustrated with respect to the large North-South wage differential that prevailed in the United States and that led to substantial out-migration of labour from the South and in-migration of firms to take advantage of the low wage labour. By the 1970s, that wage differential had disappeared when comparisons were made for the same type of labour (i.e. after controlling for human capital differences) and when comparisons were made on the bases of real wage (i.e. controlling for cost of living differences).[8]

Summary and concluding observations

Barriers to the interprovincial mobility of labour exist in various forms: professional occupational licensing; government occupational licensing of trades; preferential hiring practices; income security programs; and education and language requirements.

Unfortunately, the dramatic changes that are occurring in the Canadian labour market are creating pressures to increase barriers to interprovincial labour mobility just at the time when there is also the

---

7 Vanderkamp (1970), for example, indicates that for every 5 unemployed persons who leave the Maritimes, 2 previously *employed* people become unemployed because of multiplier effects associated with the loss of expenditures from the migrant. The net effect is a reduction in unemployment in the labour surplus region, albeit not by the full amount of the exodus of the unemployed.

8 Bellante (1979), Bishop, Formby and Thistle (1992), Coelho and Ghali (1971), and Farber and Newman (1987, 1989).

greatest need to reduce such barriers. For example, Ontario has for several years been going through a painful restructuring of its industrial base. Labour has pressured the Ontario government for protection and one result has been a move by the Ontario government to cut Quebec contractors and labourers out of the market for Ontario public works contracts. The new restrictions will create roughly 3,500 jobs for Ontario workers, at an unspecified extra cost for Ontario taxpayers (*Globe and Mail*, September 28 1993, pp. B1-B2).

Those concerned about economic progress have emphasized that barriers to interprovincial labour mobility must be removed, for several reasons: to deal with both the downside and upside adjustment problems that are increasingly occurring; to make sure our productivity performance does not slip and jeopardize our international competitiveness and our ability to sustain high-wage jobs; to foster labour mobility as a key ingredient of positive adjustment in the direction of basic market forces; to encourage marginal adjustments to reduce the necessity of disruptive inframarginal adjustments; to meet the competitive challenges posed by the free flow of labour within the EC; and to achieve the benefits of deregulation. As the cost of moving and finding jobs in other provinces fall, the artificial barriers to labour mobility become relatively more important.

The importance of reducing barriers to interprovincial labour mobility has been emphasised in a variety of recent forums. The recent Advisory Council on Adjustment (1989) identified interprovincial barriers to mobility, along with provincial standards and regulations and government procurement policies, as the significant barriers that would inhibit competitiveness and adjustment under the Canada-U.S. Free Trade Agreement. This view has been echoed by The Canada West Foundation (Duncan and Penner, 1989). The Canadian Manufacturers' Association called for the elimination of barriers through a "Canada 1993" comparable to "Europe 1992" (Rutley, 1991). A recent Gallup poll indicated that the removal of interprovincial barriers to trade was regarded as having a positive impact on competitiveness and the national economy by slightly over half of all Canadians, with only about 15 per cent regarding it as having a negative effect. Thirty per cent regarded the removal of barriers as having a positive effect on their personal economic situation, compared to 11 per cent who regarded it as having a negative effect (Bozinoff and Turcotte, 1992).

The report on Canadian Federalism and Economic Union (1991, p. 19) cited earlier work by the Macdonald Commission indicating that internal trade barriers cost Canadians upwards of 1.5 per cent of GNP. Estimates from the Canadian Manufacturers Association place the cost at just under 1 per cent of GNP, or almost $1,000 for a family of four. The report also states (p. 19) that

> These estimates do not capture the costs associated with new activity that is deterred as a result of the existence of barriers. For example, existence of internal barriers—and the knowledge that new ones can be introduced at any time—can deter Canadian businesses and entrepreneurs from undertaking new investments based on the expectation of access to the whole Canadian market. Similarly, the existence of internal barriers may discourage international investors, who seek to locate their plants in fully integrated markets, from bringing their productive investments to Canada.

The importance of removing interprovincial barriers is strongly stated in the report *Canadian Federalism and Economic Union: Partnership for Prosperity* (1991): "At the heart of efficient economic union is the free flow of people, goods, services and capital. This requires an absence of internal barriers. As barriers to international flows are coming down around the world, it is necessary now more than ever to address barriers to efficiency in our own domestic market" (p. iii), and "It is a sad irony that, in recent decades when considerable progress is being made in removing barriers to the free flow of goods and services internationally, the internal Canadian market still suffers from self-imposed internal barriers" (p. 1). Reflecting this concern, the federal government in the Throne Speech of April 1991 committed to work with the provincial governments to eliminate *internal* barriers to the flow of labour, capital and goods by 1995—a strengthening of the economic union.

While this strengthening of the *economic* union is regarded by many as an important component of strengthening the *political* union, the benefits of reducing barriers to interprovincial labour mobility exist independently of the form of political union. In the difficult search for the optimal balance of centralization and decentralization for different government functions within a federal system like Canada, reductions in the barriers to interprovincial labour mobility will confer benefits irrespective of the balance that emerges. As well, all of the stakeholders—labour, employers and consumers—can collectively gain by reducing such barriers, though there are obviously some interest groups who will experience short-run losses.

These pressure groups will exert strong influence, however, since the benefits of the barriers to interprovincial mobility are concentrated in the hands of a few, while the more sizable costs are dispersed over a larger population and often occur in intangible and indirect form. These, of course, are the classic ingredients of how protective policies are sustained even though their costs outweigh their benefits. As a recent report for a Parliamentary committee on regulation stated while looking at the broader picture of all regulations: ". . . the benefits of reform, in most cases, are widely distributed, but those who will be worse off are smaller in number, often well organized and, proportionately, stand to lose much more than those who will benefit from the reform" (Standing Committee on Finance 1992, p. 208).

What is needed is the collective will and ability to eliminate the "beggar-thy-neighbour" policies, the mutual reduction of which can make us all better off. This applies to arms reductions, tariff reductions, and reductions of the barriers to the internal mobility of goods, capital, services and labour.

References and works cited

Advisory Council on Adjustment (de Grandpre Commission). *Adjusting to Win*. Ottawa: Supply and Services, 1989.

Bellante, D. The North-South differential and the migration of heterogeneous labour. *American Economic Review*. 69 (March 1979), pp. 166-175.

Bishop, J., J. Formby and P. Thistle. Convergence of the South and Non-South income distributions, 1969-1979. *American Economic Review*. 82 (March 1992), pp. 262-272.

Boadway, R. *The Constitutional Division of Powers: An Economic Perspective*. Ottawa: Economic Council of Canada, 1992.

Bozinoff, L. and Turcotte. Canadians see little personal benefit in removing interprovincial trade barriers. *The Gallop Report*. (December 1991), pp. 1-2.

Brown, D., F. Lazar and D. Schwanen. *Free to Move: Strengthening the Canadian Economic Union*. Toronto: C.D. Howe Institute, 1992.

Canadian Federalism and Economic Union: Partnership for Prosperity. Ottawa: Supply and Services, 1991.

Coelho, P. and M. Ghali. The end of the North-South wage differential. *American Economic Review*. 61 (December 1971), pp. 932-937.

Courchene, T. Interprovincial migration and economic adjustment. *Canadian Journal of Economics*. 3 (Nov. 1970), pp. 551-576.

Courchene, T. *Migration, Income, and Employment: Canada 1965-68*. Montreal: C. D. Howe Institute, 1984.

Duncan, S. and E.T. Penner. Time for action: reducing interprovincial barriers to trade. *Western Perspectives: Canada West Foundation*. (May 1989), pp. 1-16.

Economic Council of Canada. *Employment in the Service Economy*. Ottawa: Supply and Services, 1991a.

Economic Council of Canada. *A Joint Venture: The Economics of Constitutional Options. Twenty-eighth Annual Review*. Ottawa: Economic Council of Canada, 1991b.

Employment and Immigration Canada. *Legislative/Regulatory Barriers to Interprovincial Labour Mobility.* Ottawa: CEIC Policy and Program Analysis, Strategic Policy and Planning, 1979.

Farber, S. and R. Newman. Accounting for South/Non-South real wage differentials and for changes in those differentials over time. *Review of Economics and Statistics.* 59 (May 1987), pp. 215-223.

Farber, S. and R. Newman. Regional wage differentials and the spacial convergence of worker characteristics prices. *Review of Economics and Statistics.* 71 (May 1989), pp. 224-35.

Grant, E.K. and J. Vanderkamp. The effects of migration on income: a micro study with Canadian data 1965-1981. *Canadian Journal of Economics.* 13 (August 1980), pp. 381-406.

Grant, E.K. and J. Vanderkamp. *The Economic Causes and Effects of Migration: Canada 1965-1971.* Ottawa: Economic Council of Canada, 1976.

Gunderson, M. and A. Verma. Canadian labour policy and global competition. *Canadian Business Law Journal.* 20 (March 1992), pp. 63-89.

Howse, R. Towards a high but level playing field: economic union, social justice, and constitutional reform. Toronto: Centre of Public Law and Public Policy, Osgoode Law School, 1992.

Kleiner, M., R. Gay and K. Greene. Barriers to labour migration: the case of occupational licensing. *Industrial Relations.* 21 (Fall 1982), pp. 383-391.

Laber, G. and R. Chase, Interprovincial migration in Canada as a human capital decision. *Journal of Political Economy.* 79 (July\August 1971), pp. 795-804.

Lazar, F. Labour market policies and the jurisdictional distribution of powers. In *Free to Move: Strengthening the Canadian Economic Union.* Edited by D. Brown, F. Lazar and D. Schwanen. Toronto: C.D. Howe Institute, 1992.

Lucas, R. E. Jr. On the mechanics of economic development. *Journal of Monetary Economics.* 22 (July 1988), pp. 3-22.

Macdonald, D. (Commissioner). *Royal Commission on the Economic Union and Development Prospects for Canada.* Volume 3. Ottawa: Supply and Services, 1985.

Mansell, R., and L. Copithorne. Canadian regional economic disparities: A survey. In *Disparities and Interregional Adjustment.* Toronto: University of Toronto Press, 1986.

Milne, W. *Interprovincial trade barriers: A survey and assessment.* Ottawa: Purchasing Management Association, 1987.

Muzondo, T. and B. Pazderka. *Professional Licensing and Competition Policy: Effects of Licensing on Earnings and Rates-of-Return Differentials.* Ottawa: Bureau of Competition Policy, Research Branch, 1979.

Osberg, L. and D. Gordon. Inter-regional migration and inter-industry labour mobility in Canada: The role of job availability and wage differentials. Ottawa: Employment and Immigration Canada, 1991.

Pashigian, P. Has occupational licensing reduced geographic mobility and raised earnings? In *Occupational Licensure and Regulation.* Edited by S. Rottenberg. Washington, D. C.: American Enterprise Institute, 1980.

Pashigian, P. Occupational licensing and inter-state mobility of professionals. *Journal of Law and Economics.* 22 (April, 1979), pp. 1-25.

Prosperity Secretariat. *Canada's Prosperity: Challenges and Prospects.* Ottawa: Government of Canada, 1992.

Revey and Associates. *Counteraction Procurement in the Public Sector in Canada.* Report Prepared for Industry, Science and Technology Canada, 1992.

Robinson, C. and N. Tomes. Self-selection and interprovincial migration in Canada. *Canadian Journal of Economics.* 15 (August 1982), pp. 474-502.

Romer, P. Increasing returns and long-run growth. *Journal of Political Economy.* 91 (October 1986), pp. 1002-10037.

Romer, P. Endogenous technological change. *Journal of Political Economy.* 98 (No. 5, part 2, 1990), pp. S71-S102.

Rutley, T. Canada 1993: A plan for the creation of a single economic market in Canada. Toronto: Canadian Manufacturers' Association, 1991.

Shaw, R. *Inter-Metropolitan Migration in Canada: Changing Determinants of the Three Decades.* Toronto: New Canada Publications, 1985.

Smith Gunther and Associates. *Background Notes on the Identification of Interprovincial Non-Tariff Barriers.* Report prepared for Industry, Science and Technology Canada, 1992.

Springer, B. *The Social Dimension of 1992.* New York: Greenwood Press, 1992.

Standing Committee on Finance. *Minutes of the Proceedings and Evidence of the Sub-Committee on Regulations and Competitiveness.* Ottawa: Ministry of Supply and Services, 1992.

Statistics Canada. *Mobility Status and Interprovincial Migration.* 1986 Census No. 93-108, 1989.

Thom, G. The single European market and labour mobility, *Industrial Relations Journal.* 23 (Spring 1992), pp. 14-25.

Trebilcock, M., D. Chandler and R. Howse. *Trade and Transitions.* (Toronto: University of Toronto Press: 1990).

Trebilcock, M., Kaiser and R. Prichard. Interprovincial restrictions on the mobility of resources: goods, capital and labour. In *Intergovernmental Relations: Issues and Alternatives.* Toronto: Ontario Economic Council, 1977.

Trebilcock, M., J. Whalley, C. Rogerson and I. Ness. Provincially induced trade barriers in Canada. In *Federalism and the Canadian Economic Union.* Edited by M. Trebilcock *et al.* Toronto: Ontario Economic Council and University of Toronto Press, 1983.

Vanderkamp, J. Interregional mobility in Canada. *Canadian Journal of Economics.* 1 (August 1968), pp. 595-608.

Vanderkamp, J. Return migration: Its significance and behaviour. *Western Economic Journal.* 10 (December 1971), pp. 460-466.

Vanderkamp, J. The effects of out-migration on regional employment. *Canadian Journal of Economics.* 3 (November 1970), pp. 541-549.

Vanderkamp, J. Migration flows: their determinants and the effects of return migration. *Journal of Political Economy*. 79 (September\October 1971), pp. 1012-1031.

Vanderkamp, J. The role of population size in migration studies. *Canadian Journal of Economics*. 9 (August 1976), pp. 508-516.

Vanderkamp, J. The efficiency of the interregional adjustment process. In *Disparities and Interregional Adjustment*. Edited by K. Norrie. Toronto: University of Toronto Press, 1986.

Watson, T. Interprovincial standards program—a model of flexibility and co-operation. Background paper 29. Ottawa: Federal Task Force on Skill Development Leave, 1983.

Winer, S. and D. Gauthier. *Internal Migration and Fiscal Structure*. Ottawa: Economic Council of Canada, 1982.

Big Wheels Stalling: How Bad are Barriers to Transportation Between the Provinces?

Norman Bonsor

THIS PAPER LOOKS AT THE IMPORTANT QUESTION of whether or not there are barriers to interprovincial trade in the Canadian transportation sector, and if so, how serious they are. For the purposes of this paper a barrier is defined as any artificial impediment faced by a supplier of interprovincial transport services.[1] In almost all cases, barriers to inter-provincial transport movements are directly due to rules and regula-

---

1   Taxation issues are not discussed in this paper. Both highway and rail carriers have argued that the tax load on Canadian operators is consider-ably in excess of that faced by U.S. companies. The taxation issue is an important one since any tax-induced increase in transportation costs will reduce the movement of goods. It is, however, beyond the scope of this paper because it is not an interprovincial barrier to transportation in the true sense (all goods and services encounter it to some extent.

tions enacted by governments. If cost-raising barriers are present, transportation costs will be at a sub-optimally high level, thus reducing the volume of trade between provinces and ultimately lowering real incomes for Canadians.

Governments in Canada have a very long history of intervening in transportation markets. Over the period from the early and mid-1930s to the latter part of the 1980s, federal (in the case of the railways) and provincial (in the case of highway trucking) governments have restricted competition in Canadian transportation markets and imposed other cost-raising regulations on carriers. Provincial governments, especially those in Western and Maritime Canada, have frequently complained that high transportation costs threaten the economic well-being of the provincial economies. Provincial complaints have been generally aimed at federal policies that govern railway pricing. Rail rates are asserted to be "too high" and thus federal policies are responsible for "high" transportation costs. But since the mid-1930s, provincial governments have created a bewildering hodge-podge of regulations governing the supply and provision of trucking services. Although complaining that the federal government is the prime cause of the problem may make political mileage, there has been little recognition on the part of the complainants that restraining or eliminating competition in the highway trucking industry is itself directly responsible for creating transportation costs that are "too high."

The issue of artificial barriers to the movement across provinces is not a trivial one given the transport intensity of the Canadian economy. Although measurement is very difficult, it is apparent that Canada is one of the most transport intensive economies in the world. The relatively small population base, the large distances between major centres of economic activity and the importance of natural resources in the national economy suggest the need for large expenditures on transportation inputs. Skoulas (1981), for example, estimated that operating revenues for railway freight, airline freight, water freight and for-hire and private trucking were close to 10 percent of gross national product.

The Canadian economy has frequently been characterized as being small and (increasingly) open. It is, in effect, a "price-taker" for both imports and export since Canadian producers do not have the power, individually or collectively, to set prices for either imports or exports. It has long been recognized that if a country (or a region in a country) is a price-taker with respect to both imports and exports, the presence of transportation costs reduces the price received for its exports and raises the prices paid for its imports. This means that the burden of transportation costs cannot be transferred to foreign sellers or buyers. The consequence of an increase in transportation costs is that real wages and resource rents decline (Anderson 1982). Analytically, transportation costs have the same type of impact on real incomes as do tariffs, with the important caveat that transportation costs are real while tariffs are political.

The size and nature of interprovincial trade in goods

It is very difficult to obtain reliable and current data on interprovincial trade in goods. The most recent data, released in January 1993, is for 1988 (Statistics Canada cat. 11-010). The value of interprovincial trade in goods totalled $89.35 billion. This is considerably smaller than the value of international trade in goods, which equalled approximately $159 billion. Nonetheless, interprovincial trade in goods accounted for 14.7 percent of gross domestic product in 1988. Ontario, Quebec and Alberta accounted for 80 percent of total exports, with Ontario's share alone accounting for 41 percent of total trade in goods.

Seven commodity groups accounted for over half of the interprovincial trade in goods. In order of importance these were: food and food products ($11.4 billion); metal products ($9.35 billion); chemical products ($8.3 billion); transportation equipment ($6.8 billion); electrical products ($6.6 billion); mineral fuels ($6.3 billion); and clothing and textiles ($5.7 billion).

In the case of Ontario and Quebec, exports to other provinces were highly diverse, reflecting the large industrial and agricultural bases in the two provinces. Exports from the other provinces were closely related to provincial resource bases. British Columbia exported lumber, pulp and paper and food products. Alberta's exports were highly concentrated in crude petroleum, natural gas and meat products. For Manitoba and Saskatchewan, the bulk of exports to other provinces were accounted for by food and agricultural products. Atlantic Canada's, exports (which account for only 6 percent of total interprovincial trade in

goods) included metallic ores, newsprint and electric power from Newfoundland, agricultural products and fish from Prince Edward Island,
gasoline, food products and clothing from Nova Scotia and transport
equipment, food products and paper and lumber from New Brunswick.

Only Ontario and Quebec had substantial export links to both
eastern and western Canada. The overall trading pattern has been
highly localized among neighbouring provinces (Ontario-Quebec,
Nova Scotia-New Brunswick, Saskatchewan-Alberta, Alberta-British
Columbia). The amount of trade between the western provinces and
Atlantic Canada has been very small, no doubt due to the high cost of
transporting goods over very long distances.

The transportation origin-destination data reflect the basic interprovincial trade patterns in the export and import of goods. In general, rail
movements are dominated by the long-distance transportation of bulk
and low value commodities. In contrast, highway movements between
provinces are typically for relatively high value goods.

In the case of railway movements, there are, and have been for many
years, serious directional imbalances in the demand for freight transportation in Canada. The major movement direction (the "head-haul")
is from the four western provinces to Ontario and Quebec and is largely
comprised of grain, coal and lumber shipments.[2] In sharp contrast, the
rail movements from Ontario to the west (the "back-haul") is made-up
of mixed car-load freight (including that carried in poolcars—a railcar
filled with shipments of many different products sent by different
shippers) of finished and semi-finished goods, steel and motor vehicles.
Similarly, more tonnage moves from Ontario and Quebec to the Atlantic
region than the reverse, although the imbalance is of a much lower
magnitude than is the case for Ontario and the western provinces.

In the case of highway trucking, directional imbalances are large
and have grown over time. The head-haul is from Ontario and Quebec
to Alberta and British Columbia. In recent years (1990 and 1991) approximately twice as much traffic moved to Alberta and British Columbia
from Ontario as the reverse. Manitoba and Saskatchewan to Ontario

---

2   In any given year, a large proportion of the grain tonnage moving from the
    Prairie provinces to Ontario is destined for export markets. Even if such
    tonnage is excluded, the directional balance still exists.

generated more tonnage than the reverse movement from Ontario. Quebec and Ontario generated more traffic to the Atlantic region than was the case for the Atlantic region to Quebec and Ontario.

Barriers to interprovincial highway movements

Prior to the passage of the Motor Vehicle Transport Act in 1988, the federal government effectively ceded control of interprovincial highway transportation to the provinces, even though interprovincial (but not intraprovincial) highway movements are a federal responsibility under the British North America Act.

In the early 1930s there was a considerable demand for the industry to be regulated. First, the two major rail carriers (who were running substantial losses partly as a result of the depressed level of economic activity) faced increasing competition in the short and medium-haul freight market from highway carriers, to which they sought a political solution. The rail carriers wanted the federal government to regulate the trucking industry by strictly controlling entry and also to set rates for highway movements at the same level as the prevailing rail class rates. Adoption of this policy would have almost completely eliminated competition between rail and highway carriers. Second, the established sector of the trucking industry also demanded regulation but wanted it at the provincial rather than federal level. Essentially, existing highway carriers wanted the provinces to regulate (prohibit) entry while at the same time being free to set rates at a level that allowed them to compete with rail.

By the latter part of the 1930s, many provinces were regulating entry not only for intraprovincial highway movements but also extraprovincially (between Canada and the U.S. and interprovincially). In 1937 and again in 1940, the Federal government introduced legislation to regulate the interprovincial trucking industry. The major rationale for this legislation was the fear that a patch-work of differing rules and regulations would arise. Both bills were withdrawn in the face of strong opposition from the provinces and the industry. Anyway, federal coverage would only have extended to the extraprovincial sector of the industry, which at that time accounted for only 3-5 percent of the industry (Currie, 1967).

In 1949, the Supreme Court of Canada ruled (and was later upheld by the British Privy Council) that provinces had no powers under the British North America Act to interfere with extraprovincial movements. The decision effectively extended federal jurisdiction to the total operations of any transport firm that engaged in interprovincial trade. But the federal government formally delegated its constitutional power over interprovincial and international trucking operations to the provinces by passing the 1954 Motor Vehicle Transport Act.

Regulation as practised by the provinces did indeed create a crazy-quilt pattern of rules. All provinces regulated entry into the interprovincial and international trucking industry. One province (Newfoundland) even attempted to regulate rates. All provinces except Alberta regulated entry into the intraprovincial industry. Regulatory boards restricted the amount of competition in markets for trucking services by restricting the entry of new carriers and by greatly limiting the ability of existing firms to expand services. Since restricting entry limits the amount of competition and enables rate levels to be set at a level higher than that which would prevail in a non-regulated competitive market, it thus provided a clear benefit to those carriers that had managed to enter the industry. In essence, entry regulation created specific "rights" to flows of above-normal profits (profits over and above those available in a competitive market). In many provinces, the "right" conferred on a licence holder was tradeable. In Ontario, for example, there was a brisk trade in licences. In 1975, part of an authority to haul lumber was sold for $200,000.[3] In addition to restricting entry, Manitoba and Saskatchewan actively regulated rate levels, Quebec and British Columbia "approved" file rates and others merely required rates to be filed.

Entry regulation in the majority of provinces was based on a public necessity and convenience test or a public interest test. The term "public necessity and convenience" or "public interest" is one that lacks any objective interpretation. Decisions of regulatory boards were highly unpredictable and seemingly capricious. In only a minority of cases

---

3 The value of a licence on the open market would be equal to its capitalized value, which in turn would be equal to the discounted present value of anticipated monopoly profits. If entry were not restricted, the value of an existing licence would equal zero.

were reasons for decisions given or published. The regulatory boards were to a large extent "captured" by the established entrants. Stigler (1971) has argued that producers essentially "capture" regulatory boards. Regulatory boards in making decisions serve the established producers and not the public interest. The "capture" theory holds that regulatory boards generally end up "protecting" the established producers from consumers. An excellent example of this was the UPS application for a licence in Ontario: the Ontario Highway Transport had counsel for a major group of shippers opposed to the application actually write the decision denying UPS a licence.[4]

A major problem is that for much of the period in question, provincial regulatory boards viewed interprovincial trucking as being merely an extension of intraprovincial trucking and subject to the same rules. A trucking company wishing to operate a service from Toronto to Vancouver, for example, would (if he wanted to drop off or pick up freight in each province along the way) have to obtain an operating permit in all five provinces. This meant five applications and five hearings. The hearing process was very expensive. Those seeking entry to the industry and those attempting to block entry employed lawyers to argue the case and in addition paraded witnesses before the regulatory board to testify either that the services of the entrant were desperately needed or that the market was already being served by those attempting to block entry. In the early 1980s, the daily cost to an applicant for a hearing before a highway regulatory board was in excess of $2,000 (excluding the cost to the applicant of having senior management tied up in the hearing process) and many hearings lasted for 10 days or more.

Even if an applicant did manage to obtain entry, conditions on permits across provinces were typically not the same. Permits were

---

4   In 1979 UPS applied for a licence in Ontario and was opposed by 147 respondents. In the course of a 10 month hearing, UPS called 352 witnesses and the respondents 363 witnesses. When it became public knowledge that the decision to reject the application was written by one of the counsel for the respondents, the Ontario cabinet ordered the application reheard and UPS was subsequently granted a licence. The cost of the hearings was estimated to be in excess of $3 million.

generally highly restrictive and limited operations to specific routes and/or specific commodities. A carrier with an operating authority on the Toronto-Winnipeg lane for general freight, for example, might not be allowed to back-haul specified commodities or extend service to points other than Toronto and Winnipeg. Carriers with a permit to operate between Toronto and Vancouver might or might not be allowed to drop off or pick up freight in Regina or Winnipeg.

These restrictions on licences in and of themselves clearly raised transportation costs.[5] Carriers were forced to operate with unbalanced loads (running empty on some traffic lanes) due to an inability to compete for traffic. In addition to the restrictions placed on licences, the public necessity and convenience test was used to restrict the supply of carriers on any given traffic lane. The restrictions on the number of carriers allowed in a given market reduced the level of competition and directly raised trucking rates. In those markets for which rail and highway carriers competed for traffic, the limits set by regulation on competition in the trucking industry allowed rail carriers (who were required to set rates jointly and so there was no competition between rail carriers) to set prices at a level higher than that which would have prevailed in the absence of regulation of the trucking industry.

Disparities in the regulation of the industry across provinces developed into a significant concern for shippers and others in the mid-1960s, so much so that the federal government enacted and proclaimed Part

---

5   There have been a large number of studies showing that the type of entry regulation practised in the trucking industry raises production costs. There are four main reasons. First, restrictions placed on licences that limited the number of routes served and commodities carried increase the level of empty back-hauls. Second, by limiting competition, entry regulation creates conditions in which labour unions are able to raise wages above those that would have occurred in the absence of regulation. Boucher (1980), for example, estimates that regulation in Quebec resulted in labour costs being increased by approximately 18 percent. Third, carriers commit resources to entry-seeking and forestalling activity. Bonsor (1980) estimates that in Ontario trucking industry, entry-seeking and forestalling activities accounted for 2.1 percent of annual operating revenues. Fourth, in markets where entry is restricted carriers may suffer from "X inefficiency" (sloppy management).

III of the 1967 National Transportation Act reasserting federal control over interprovincial trucking. Then the provinces promised to harmonize regulations, with the result that Part III was not implemented. However, the provinces did little in the way of harmonizing regulations. Eventually, in response to growing pressures from the federal government and shippers, provincial transportation ministers (some very reluctantly) signed an understanding in 1985 to replace the public necessity and convenience test with a reverse onus test.[6] The reverse onus test essentially assumes that entry is in the public interest, and those wishing to block entry bear the burden of proving otherwise. The ministers also agreed to "eventually" drop prohibitions on entry except for a fitness test.

The 1987 Motor Vehicle Transport Act (effective January 1, 1988) introduced a homogenous "fitness only" test for entry into the interprovincial trucking industry. That is, any carrier able to offer proof of adequate insurance etc. would automatically be granted a licence. A five year transition period was allowed. During this five year period, regulatory decisions on entry would be made using the reverse onus test.

A number of provinces, including Alberta and Quebec, granted all applications as a matter of policy during the transition period. Others only partially adopted an open entry policy.[7] Manitoba and New Brunswick, on the other hand, attempted to carry on regulating entry as if nothing very much had been changed by the 1987 legislation. Both

---

6   In 1980, the U.S. passed the Motor Carrier Act effectively eliminating economic regulation of the industry. Large numbers of Canadian-domiciled carriers took advantage of the eased-entry regime and expanded operations in the U.S. American carriers lobbied for "mirror" reciprocity: an open entry regime in Canada. In 1982, the U.S. placed a moratorium on issuing further permits to Canadian carriers, later lifted when the Canadian government agreed "in principle" to open borders for international truck movements. In addition to the pressure placed on the provinces by the federal government to open entry into the industry, shippers saw highway rates falling in the U.S. as a result of deregulation and wanted similar benefits in Canada.

7   Saskatchewan rejected two applications for broad general freight operating authorities in 1990 and British Columbia rejected an application from an automobile carrier, also in 1990.

provinces introduced the curious notion of cumulative effect as a decision variable. In deciding whether or not to issue a licence the regulatory board would look at not only the impact that the particular applicant's entry would have on the market but also the impact that granting similar permits to other applicants would have. The cumulative effect notion was fortunately struck down by the courts.[8] If it had not been, established carriers would gave been able to argue that the cumulative effect of entry was contrary to the "public" interest, and regulatory boards would have been more able to refuse entry to new carriers.

The 1987 reforms have considerably reduced barriers to interprovincial highway movements. Provinces can no longer practice the type of entry-deterring regulation in the interprovincial sector of the industry that was prevalent prior to the reforms. It must be noted, however, that the reforms did not apply to the intraprovincial industry. A number of provinces (Ontario and Quebec for example) opened provincial trucking markets to competition by eliminating restrictions on entry or by following a liberalized entry regime.[9] But in other provinces, especially Manitoba and to a lesser extent Saskatchewan, entry of new carriers or expansion by existing carriers is still subject to entry deterring regulation. A carrier obtaining an interprovincial licence for the Toronto-Winnipeg lane, for example, would not be able to pick up traffic in Winnipeg and run to Brandon (Manitoba) without first obtaining an intraprovincial permit. Since Manitoba still has a public necessity and convenience test for intraprovincial licences, the application can easily be refused.

The available evidence suggests that trucking rates have declined over the period 1988-1992 in response to increased competition in both inter and intraprovincial markets. The annual reviews of the National Transportation Agency indicate that rate increases have been below the rate of inflation. Transport Canada, in the comprehensive Motor Vehicle

---

8   *R. Lindsay and G. Smith vs The Motor Transport Board of Manitoba, Arnold Bros. Transport Ltd. and al.*, Court of Appeal of Manitoba, September 8, 1989.

9   In April 1991, the NDP government in Ontario in response to complaints from carriers that rate levels had fallen "below cost" prohibited the issuance of new entry permits in the intraprovincial sector for a 2 year period. The moratorium on new intraprovincial entry permits expired on April 25, 1993.

Transport Act review document, shows that real freight rates in the highway sector declined an average of 17 percent between 1986 and 1988.[10]

The major remaining barriers to interprovincial highway carrier movements are in relation to "non-economic" rules and regulations, particularly with respect to differing length standards for highway trailers. The most significant cost-raising regulation is in Ontario and relates to the maximum permissable trailer length. In all the Western provinces and all but 4 U.S. states (Alaska, Connecticut, Hawaii and Rhode Island), maximum vehicle length has been set at 25 metres and maximum trailer length at 53 feet. In Ontario, the maximum vehicle length is 23 metres and maximum trailer length is 48 feet.[11] Quebec allows 51 foot trailers and the other eastern provinces have the same standard as Ontario.

Carriers supplying services between Ontario and the west (and Ontario and the U.S.) are thus faced with either switching equipment at the Ontario-Manitoba border or sizing the equipment for the lowest common standard. Given that switching equipment is rarely practical (unloading and reloading would be required), carriers are forced to run smaller units in the Ontario-West markets. The influence of the Ontario position on length is likely to exert a significant influence on highway markets outside Ontario. Given that more shipments originate in Ontario than in any other province (Ontario accounted for 41 percent of interprovincial trade in goods in 1988), carriers have an incentive to buy equipment that meets the lowest common length restriction for use in

---

10   It should be noted that a number of jurisdictions "liberalized" entry requirements ahead of the legislation.

11   The Ontario government has refused to allow an increase in length in Ontario, ostensibly on safety grounds. It must be noted that there is considerable opposition to increasing the length limitations from groups such as automobile clubs and associations who believe that increasing the allowable length would increase the number of highway accidents. The issue of whether or not to increase the lengths allowed in Ontario is under active consideration by the Ontario Ministry of Transportation. The major groups pressing for an increase to 53 feet for trailers are trailer equipment manufacturers, shippers, and the trucking industry.

all markets. This clearly raises the cost of moving freight in and out of Ontario and elsewhere, since carriers must operate with lower cubic capacity (less space available in the trailer). An increase to 53 feet in allowable trailer length in Ontario, from the existing 48 feet, would increase cubic carrying capacity by roughly 10 percent and would lead to a non-trivial reduction in the cost of producing line-haul services.

The Conference Board of Canada (1992) details 50 case studies of companies facing barriers to interprovincial trade. Nine of the case studies focus on companies engaged in interprovincial for-hire trucking and on an additional two companies that have significant private trucking operations. All nine for-hire trucking companies complained of the differing length and weight standards across provinces (as did the private carriers), with almost all highlighting the refusal of Ontario to permit the longer vehicle and trailer lengths. A number of carriers confirmed that they acquired equipment that would meet the most stringent maximum length standards for use in all markets. In addition, the majority of the companies also pointed to the fact that there was no uniformity in the interpretation and administration by the provinces of national safety standards, especially with respect to maintenance.

The report of the National Transportation Review Commission (1993) recommends that if the six provinces east of the Manitoba/Ontario border do not voluntarily adopt what the commission perceives as a Canada-U.S. common standard on length by March 31, 1994, the federal government should impose one.[12]

Barriers to interprovincial rail movements

Interprovincial rail movements are federally regulated and are thus not subject to provincial regulation. Provinces have the legal authority to regulate the operations of a railway that operates only intraprovincially.

The 1987 National Transportation Act provided for the establishment of independent shortline railways. An existing carrier could transfer an uneconomical line to a (potentially) lower cost independent

12   The Ontario government announced in July, 1993 that it intends to introduce legislation allowing for the longer lengths.

operator rather than abandon the line. A line that is uneconomical for a major carrier such as Canadian National or Canadian Pacific may be economical if operated by a lower cost operator. The major cost advantage that a shortline operator has over Canadian National and Canadian Pacific is in labour costs. The lower labour costs are directly attributable to flexible work rules, smaller crew manning requirements and, in some cases, lower wage and benefit levels.

In December, 1990 the Supreme Court of Canada ruled that Canadian National could convey the Stettler (Alberta) subdivision to the newly formed Central Western Railway. At issue was the question of whether or not the Central Western was subject to federal labour legislation in the operation of the shortline. The Canadian Labour Relations Board had ruled (and been upheld in the Federal Court of Appeal) that union successor rights were in operation and thus the Central Western Railway was bound to operate under the agreement negotiated between the Union and Canadian National. The Supreme Court ruled that the shortline did not constitute a federal undertaking since it was not an interprovincial railway and in addition that it was not an integral part of a "core" federal undertaking. Thus the shortline operator was not bound by the union contract and could introduce flexible work rules and changes to wage and benefit rates.

There are two shortlines currently operating in Canada: the Central Western referred to above and the Goderich and Exeter Railway Co. which operates between Goderich and Stratford (Ontario). Both lines, which were previously judged uneconomical, are now profitable. Both have benefited from flexible manning procedures and work rules and so production costs have declined under new ownership. In the case of the Goderich and Exeter, which has been very aggressive in competing for business from highway carriers, labour inputs have been reduced by approximately 40 percent under the new ownership.

Under existing legislation and jurisprudence, an interprovincial railway would almost certainly come under the jurisdiction of the Canadian Labour Relations Board and in consequence be subject to union successor rights. Given the "spanish" practices (rules and work procedures that lead to overmanning) which are embedded in existing labour contracts between the railways and the rail unions, it is very doubtful that any operator could successfully operate a shortline interprovincially without obtaining significant changes in the existing union agreements. The existence of successor rights in at least one important case will very likely mean that a potentially economical interprovincial line will be abandoned rather than conveyed to a shortline operator. In 1992, Canadian Pacific applied to the National Transportation Agency for permission to abandon all its lines east of Sherbrooke, Quebec. These lines, comprising 700 kilometres of track of the Canadian Atlantic Railway, extend from Sherbrooke across Maine to St. John, New Brunswick. One of the prime reasons that Canadian Pacific is seeking to abandon the line rather than convert it to a shortline operator is that although it is potentially economically viable under realistic work rules and staffing levels, the mandated successor rights do not allow for the required flexibility. Thus a potentially viable interprovincial rail line will be abandoned rather than operated as a shortline, harming all regional residents.

It should be noted that even the formation of purely intraprovincial shortline railways under existing rules and regulations is difficult. In Ontario and British Columbia labour laws make it very difficult or impossible to introduce the required flexibility in work rules and manning practices.[13]

Summary

Interprovincial trade in goods accounts for close to 15 percent of gross domestic product. We have argued that barriers to interprovincial trade in the transportation sector have declined substantially since 1988. The major barrier was that the federal government allowed provinces to regulate entry into the interprovincial trucking industry. Provincial regulatory activity significantly reduced competition and raised costs for interprovincial highway movements. The 1987 Motor Vehicle Transport Act significantly reduced the artificial regulatory barriers.

The major barrier that still exists in 1993 in the highway sector is the lack of uniformity across Canada in the maximum vehicle length. 53 feet trailers are standard in the western provinces and in all but 4 U.S. states.

---

13   The Goderich and Exeter was formed prior to changes in Ontario labour laws.

There is a significant body of evidence to show that the limitation to 48 feet in Ontario and the Atlantic provinces has raised the cost of interprovincial highway movements.

In the case of railways, the biggest barrier is the limits placed on the conveyance of interprovincial trackage to a shortline operator. It is highly unlikely that an interprovincial shortline would not be subject to union successor rights under existing legislation. This means that the required flexibility in manning levels and work rules could not be achieved and thus major increases in productivity could not be achieved. Carriers will therefore abandon interprovincial trackage (as Canadian Pacific has applied to do with the Canadian Atlantic Railway) rather than attempt to convey the track to a shortline operator.

Bibliography

Anderson, F.J. 1982. "Transport Costs and Real Incomes In a Small Region." *Canadian Journal of Economics* 15, pp. 525-34.

Bonsor, N. 1980. "The Impact of Regulation on For-Hire Carriers." In *Studies in Trucking Regulation*. Ottawa: Economic Council of Canada.

Boucher, M. 1980. "Regulation of the Quebec Trucking Industry: Institutions, Practices and Analytical Considerations." In *Studies in Trucking Regulation*. Ottawa: Economic Council of Canada.

Conference Board of Canada. 1992. *Barriers to Inter-provincial Trade: Fifty Case Studies*. Toronto.

Currie, A.W. 1967. *Canadian Transportation Economics*. Toronto: University of Toronto Press.

National Transportation Agency. Various Years. *Annual Review*. Ottawa: National Transportation Agency.

National Transportation Review Commission. 1993. *Competition in Transportation: Policy and Legislation in Review*. Ottawa: Supply and Services Canada.

Skoulas, N. 1981. *Transport Costs and Their Implications for Price Competitiveness in Canadian Goods Producing Industries*. Ottawa: Consumer and Corporate Affairs.

Statistics Canada 1993. "Canada's Interprovincial Trade Flows of Goods 1984-88." *Canadian Economic Observer*, January. Ottawa: Statistics Canada.

Stigler, G. 1971. "The Theory of Economic Regulation." *Bell Journal of Economics and Management Science* 2, pp. 3-9.